Embedded Linux Development using Yocto Projects

Second Edition

Learn to leverage the power of Yocto Project to build efficient
Linux-based products

Otavio Salvador
Daiane Angolini

BIRMINGHAM - MUMBAI

Embedded Linux Development using Yocto Projects

Second Edition

First published: July 2014

Second edition: November 2017

Production reference: 1141117

Published by Packt Publishing Ltd.
Livery Place
35 Livery Street
Birmingham
B3 2PB, UK.

ISBN: 978-1-78847-046-9

www.packtpub.com

Credits

Authors
Otavio Salvador
Daiane Angolini

Reviewer
Radek Dostal

Acquisition Editor
Prateek Bharadwaj

Content Development Editor
Nikita Pawar

Technical Editor
Manish D Shanbhag

Copy Editors
Safis Editing
Juliana Nair

Project Coordinator
Judie Jose

Proofreader
Safis Editing

Indexer
Rekha Nair

Graphics
Tanya Dutta

Production Coordinator
Nilesh Mohite

About the Authors

Otavio Salvador loves technology and started his free software activities in 1999. In 2002, he founded O.S. Systems, a company focused on embedded system development services and consultancy worldwide, creating and maintaining customized BSPs and helping companies with their product development challenges. This resulted in him joining the OpenEmbedded community in 2008, where he became an active contributor to the OpenEmbedded project.

Daiane Angolini has been working with embedded Linux since 2008. She has been working as an application engineer at NXP, acting on internal development, porting custom applications from Android, and on-site customer support for i.MX architectures in areas such as Linux kernel, u-boot, Android, Yocto Project, and user space applications. However, it was on the Yocto Project that she found her place.

About the Reviewer

Radek Dostal is a fan of Linux and has been using it for the last 15 years. During his exchange studies in the US, he acquired a passion for embedded systems, and combining Linux with embedded systems has been his bread and butter ever since. Yocto has had a great impact on Radek's work: he managed to convince his team and managers to switch to Yocto for an important project, which built a solid foundation for several successful follow-up projects. Radek likes to contribute to open source projects as part of his work, as well as during his free time. However, if the weather is good during the weekend, you are most likely to find him in the mountains.

www.PacktPub.com

For support files and downloads related to your book, please visit www.PacktPub.com. Did you know that Packt offers eBook versions of every book published, with PDF and ePub files available? You can upgrade to the eBook version at www.PacktPub.com and as a print book customer, you are entitled to a discount on the eBook copy. Get in touch with us at service@packtpub.com for more details. At www.PacktPub.com, you can also read a collection of free technical articles, sign up for a range of free newsletters and receive exclusive discounts and offers on Packt books and eBooks.

https://www.packtpub.com/mapt

Get the most in-demand software skills with Mapt. Mapt gives you full access to all Packt books and video courses, as well as industry-leading tools to help you plan your personal development and advance your career.

Why subscribe?

- Fully searchable across every book published by Packt
- Copy and paste, print, and bookmark content
- On demand and accessible via a web browser

Customer Feedback

Thanks for purchasing this Packt book. At Packt, quality is at the heart of our editorial process. To help us improve, please leave us an honest review on this book's Amazon page at `https://www.amazon.com/dp/178847046X`.

If you'd like to join our team of regular reviewers, you can email us at `customerreviews@packtpub.com`. We award our regular reviewers with free eBooks and videos in exchange for their valuable feedback. Help us be relentless in improving our products!

Table of Contents

Preface   1

Chapter 1: Meeting the Yocto Project   7

    What is the Yocto Project?   7
    Delineating the Yocto Project   8
    Understanding Poky   9
    Using BitBake   9
    OpenEmbedded-Core   10
    Metadata   10
    The alliance of the OpenEmbedded Project and the Yocto Project   10
    Summary   11

Chapter 2: Baking Our Poky-Based System   13

    Configuring a host system   13
        Installing Poky on Debian   14
        Installing Poky on Fedora   14
    Downloading the Poky source code   15
    Preparing the build environment   16
    Knowing the local.conf file   16
    Building a target image   17
    Running images in QEMU   18
    Summary   20

Chapter 3: Using Toaster to Bake an Image   21

    What is Toaster?   21
    Installing Toaster   22
    Starting Toaster   22
    Building an image to QEMU   23
    Summary   29

Chapter 4: Grasping the BitBake Tool   31

    Understanding the BitBake tool   31
    Exploring metadata   32
    Parsing metadata   33
    Dependencies   34
    Preferring and providing recipes   35
    Fetching the source code   36

Remote file downloads   36
Git repositories   37
Optimizing the source code download   38
Disabling network access   40
Understanding BitBake's tasks   40
Extending tasks   42
Generating a root filesystem image   42
Summary   44

Chapter 5: Detailing the Temporary Build Directory   45

Detailing the build directory   45
Constructing the build directory   46
Exploring the temporary build directory   47
Understanding the work directory   48
Understanding the sysroot directories   50
Summary   52

Chapter 6: Assimilating Packaging Support   53

Using supported package formats   53
List of supported package formats   53
Choosing a package format   54
Running code during package installation   55
Understanding shared state cache   57
Explaining package versioning   58
Specifying runtime package dependencies   58
Package feeds   59
Using package feeds   61
Summary   63

Chapter 7: Diving into BitBake Metadata   65

Using metadata   65
Working with metadata   66
The basic variable setting   66
Variable expansion   66
Setting a default value using ?=   67
Setting a default value using ??=   67
Immediate variable expansion   68
Appending and prepending   68
Override syntax operators   69
Conditional metadata set   69
Conditional appending   70

File inclusion	70
Python variable expansion	71
Defining executable metadata	71
Defining Python functions in the global namespace	72
The inheritance system	72
Summary	73
Chapter 8: Developing with the Yocto Project	75
Deciphering the software development kit	75
Working with the Poky SDK	76
Using an image-based SDK	76
Generic SDK – meta-toolchain	78
Using an SDK	78
Developing applications on the target	79
Integrating with Eclipse	80
Summary	81
Chapter 9: Debugging with the Yocto Project	83
Differentiating metadata and application debugging	83
Tracking image, package, and SDK contents	84
Debugging packaging	85
Logging information during task execution	86
Utilizing a development shell	87
Using the GNU Project Debugger for debugging	89
Summary	90
Chapter 10: Exploring External Layers	91
Powering flexibility with layers	91
Detailing the layer's source code	94
Adding meta layers	96
The Yocto Project layer ecosystem	97
Summary	98
Chapter 11: Creating Custom Layers	99
Making a new layer	99
Adding metadata to the layer	101
Creating an image	102
Adding a package recipe	104
Automatically creating a base package recipe using recipetool	105
Adding support to a new machine definition	108
Wrapping an image for your machine	109

Using a custom distribution	111
MACHINE_FEATURES versus DISTRO_FEATURES	113
Understanding the variables scope	114
Summary	114

Chapter 12: Customizing Existing Recipes 115

Common use cases	115
Adding extra options to recipes based on Autoconf	116
Applying a patch	116
Adding extra files to the existing packages	117
Understanding file searching paths	117
Changing recipe feature configuration	118
Customizing BusyBox	119
Customizing the linux-yocto framework	119
Summary	121

Chapter 13: Achieving GPL Compliance 123

Understanding copyleft	123
Copyleft compliance versus proprietary code	124
Some guidelines for license compliance	124
Managing software licensing with Poky	124
Commercial licenses	125
Using Poky to achieve copyleft compliance	126
License auditing	126
Providing the source code	127
Providing compilation scripts and source code modifications	128
Providing license text	129
Summary	129

Chapter 14: Booting Our Custom Embedded Linux 131

Exploring the boards	132
Discovering the right BSP layer	133
Baking for the hardware	133
Baking for BeagleBone Black	135
Baking for Raspberry Pi 3	136
Baking for the Wandboard	137
Booting our baked image	138
Booting BeagleBone Black from the SD card	139
Booting Raspberry Pi 3 from the SD card	139
Booting Wandboard from the SD card	139
Next steps	140

Summary   141

Index   143

Preface

In the current technology trend, Linux is the next big thing. Linux has consistently released cutting-edge open source products, and Embedded Systems have been wrought in the technological portfolio of mankind.

The Yocto Project is in an optimal position to be the choice for your projects, and it provides a rich set of tools to help you use most of your energy and resources in your product development, instead of reinventing the wheel.

The usual tasks and requirements of Embedded Linux-based products and development teams were the guideline for this book's conception. Being written by active community members, with a practical and straightforward approach, it is a stepping stone for both your learning curve and the product's project.

What this book covers

Chapter 1, *Meeting the Yocto Project,* presents the first concepts and premises to introduce parts of the Yocto Project and their main tools.

Chapter 2, *Baking Our Poky-Based System,* introduces the environment needed for the first build.

Chapter 3, *Using Toaster to Bake an Image,* shows the user-friendly web interface that can be used as a wrapper for configuration and as a build tool.

Chapter 4, *Grasping the BitBake Tool,* presents the BitBake tool and how it manages the tasks and its dependencies.

Chapter 5, *Detailing the Temporary Build Directory,* details the temporary output folder of a build.

Chapter 6, *Assimilating Packaging Support,* explains the packaging mechanism used as base to create and manage all the binary packages.

Chapter 7, *Diving into BitBake Metadata,* details the BitBake metadata language which will be used for all the other chapters.

Chapter 8, *Developing with the Yocto Project,* demonstrates the workflow needed to obtain a development environment.

`Chapter` 9, *Debugging with the Yocto Project,* shows how to use Poky to generate a debug environment and how to use it.

`Chapter` 10, *Exploring External Layers,* explores one of the most important concepts of the Yocto Project—the flexibility of using external layers.

`Chapter` 11, *Creating Custom Layers,* practices the steps on layers creation.

`Chapter` 12, *Customizing Existing Recipes,* presents examples on how to customize the existing recipes.

`Chapter` 13, *Achieving GPL Compliance,* summarizes the tasks and concepts involved for a copyleft compliance product.

`Chapter` 14, *Booting Our Custom Embedded Linux,* uses real hardware machines together with the Yocto Project's tools.

What you need for this book

To understand this book better, it is important that you have some previous background about some topics which are not covered or are just briefly mentioned along the text, such as Git and Linux Kernel general knowledge, and basic compilation process.

In order to understand the big picture of the Yocto Project before going to the technical concepts detailed in this book, we recommend the open sourced booklet, *Heading for the Yocto Project,* found under the Git repository at *https://git.io/vFUiI*; the content of this booklet is intended to help newcomers to gain a better understanding of the goals of the Yocto Project and its potential uses, and it intends to provide an overview of the project, before diving into the technical details on how things can be done.

A basic understanding of the use of the GNU/Linux environment and Embedded Linux is required as well as that of the general concepts used in development such as compilation, debugging, deployment, and installation. Some experience with Shell Script and Python is a bonus, because these programming languages are core technologies used extensively by the Yocto Project's tools.

You shouldn't take any missing concepts—of those we enumerated above—as a deterrent, but as something you can learn and at the same time, practice its use, with this book. However, if you prefer to learn more about those topics, we recommend the book *Mastering Embedded Linux Programming, ISBN: 9781787283282,* by *Chris Simmonds.*

Any concept enumerated above, should not discourage you from reading this book because these can be learned concurrently.

Who this book is for

This book is intended for engineers and enthusiasts with an Embedded Linux experience, willing to learn the Yocto Project's tools for evaluation, comparison, or use in a project. This book is aimed to get you up to sprint quickly and to prevent you from getting trapped into the usual learning curve pitfalls.

Conventions

In this book, you will find many styles of text that distinguish between different kinds of information. Here are some examples of these styles, and an explanation of their meaning.

A block of code is set as follows:

```
[default]
 T = "123"
 A := "${B} ${A} test ${T}"
 T = "456"
 B = "${T} bval"
 C = "cval"
 C := "${C}append"
```

When we wish to draw your attention to a specific part of a code block, the relevant lines or items are set in bold:

```
[default]
 T = "123"
 A := "${B} ${A} test ${T}"
 T = "456"
 B = "${T} bval"
 C = "cval"
 C := "${C}append"
```

Any command-line input or output is written as follows:

```
$ sudo apt-get install gawk wget git-core diffstat unzip texinfo build-essential chrpath
```

New terms and **important words** are shown in bold. Words that you see on the screen, for example, in menus or dialog boxes, appear in the text like this: "After that, click the **Image Recipes** tab to choose the image you want to build. "

 Warnings or important notes appear in a box like this.

 Tips and tricks appear like this.

Reader feedback

Feedback from our readers is always welcome. Let us know what you think about this book—what you liked or may have disliked. Reader feedback is important for us to develop titles that you really get the most out of.

To send us general feedback, simply send an email to `feedback@packtpub.com`, and mention the book title via the subject of your message.

If there is a topic that you have expertise in and you are interested in either writing or contributing to a book, see our author guide on `www.packtpub.com/authors`.

Customer support

Now that you are the proud owner of a Packt book, we have a number of things to help you to get the most from your purchase.

Downloading the color images of this book

We also provide you with a PDF file that has color images of the screenshots/diagrams used in this book. The color images will help you better understand the changes in the output. You can download this file from `https://www.packtpub.com/sites/default/files/downloads/EmbeddedLinuxDevelopmentusingYoctoProjectsSecondEdition_ColorImages.pdf`.

Errata

Although we have taken every care to ensure the accuracy of our content, mistakes do happen. If you find a mistake in one of our books—maybe a mistake in the text or the code—we would be grateful if you would report this to us. By doing so, you can save other readers from frustration and help us improve subsequent versions of this book. If you find any errata, please report them by visiting http://www.packtpub.com/submit-errata, selecting your book, clicking on the errata submission form link, and entering the details of your errata. Once your errata are verified, your submission will be accepted and the errata will be uploaded on our website, or added to any list of existing errata, under the Errata section of that title. Any existing errata can be viewed by selecting your title from http://www.packtpub.com/support.

Piracy

Piracy of copyright material on the Internet is an ongoing problem across all media. At Packt, we take the protection of our copyright and licenses very seriously. If you come across any illegal copies of our works, in any form, on the Internet, please provide us with the location address or website name immediately so that we can pursue a remedy.

Please contact us at copyright@packtpub.com with a link to the suspected pirated material.

We appreciate your help in protecting our authors, and our ability to bring you valuable content.

Questions

You can contact us at questions@packtpub.com if you are having a problem with any aspect of the book, and we will do our best to address it.

1
Meeting the Yocto Project

In this chapter we will be introduced to the **Yocto Project**. The main concepts of the project, which are constantly used throughout the book, are discussed here. We will discuss the Yocto Project history, OpenEmbedded, Poky, BitBake, and metadata in brief, so fasten your seat belt and welcome aboard!

What is the Yocto Project?

The Yocto Project is a Linux Foundation workgroup defined as:

> *"The Yocto Project provides open source, high-quality infrastructure and tools to help developers create their own custom Linux distributions for any hardware architecture, across multiple market segments. The Yocto Project is intended to provide a helpful starting point for developers."*

The Yocto Project is an open source collaboration project that provides templates, tools, and methods to help us create custom Linux-based systems for embedded products regardless of the hardware architecture. Being managed by a Linux Foundation fellow, the project remains independent of its member organizations that participate in various ways and provide resources to the project.

It was founded in 2010 as a collaboration of many hardware manufacturers, open source operating systems, vendors, and electronics companies in an effort to reduce their work duplication, provide resources and information catering to both new and experienced users.

Among these resources is OpenEmbedded-Core, the core system component, provided by the OpenEmbedded project.

The Yocto Project is, therefore, a community open source project that aggregates several companies, communities, projects, and tools, gathering people with the same purpose to build Linux-based embedded products; all these components are in the same boat, being driven by its community needs to work together.

Delineating the Yocto Project

To ease our understanding of the duties and outcomes provided by the Yocto Project, we can use the analogy of a computing machine. The input is a set of data that describes what we want, that is, our specification. As an output, we have the desired Linux-based embedded product.

If the output is a product running a Linux-based operating system, the result generated is the pieces that compose the operating system, such as the Linux kernel, bootloader, and the root filesystem (`rootfs`) bundle which are properly organized.

To produce the resultant `rootfs` bundle and other deliverables, the Yocto Project's tools are present in all intermediary steps. The reuse of previously built utilities and other software components are maximized while building other applications, libraries, and any other software components in the right order and with the desired configuration, including the fetching of the required source code from their respective repositories, such as The Linux Kernel Archives (`www.kernel.org`), GitHub, and `www.SourceForge.net`.

The Yocto Project's tools prepare its own build environment, utilities, and toolchain, reducing the amount of host software dependency. A subtle but important implication is that the determinism is considerably increased as the utilities and their versions as well as their configuration options are the same, thus minimizing the number of host utilities to rely on and producing the same result independent of the host Linux distribution being used.

We can list some projects, such as Poky, BitBake, and OpenEmbedded-Core, under the Yocto Project umbrella, all of them being complementary and playing specific roles in the system. We will understand exactly how they work together in this chapter and throughout the book.

Understanding Poky

Poky is the Yocto Project reference system and is composed of a collection of tools and metadata. It is platform-independent and performs cross-compiling, using the BitBake tool, OpenEmbedded Core, and a default set of metadata, as shown in the following figure. It provides the mechanism to build and combine thousands of distributed open source projects to form a fully customizable, complete, and coherent Linux software stack.

Poky's main objective is to provide all the features an embedded developer needs.

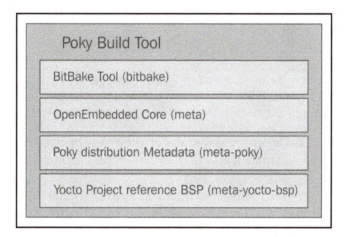

Using BitBake

BitBake is a task scheduler that parses Python and shell script mixed code. The code parsed generates and runs tasks, which are basically a set of steps ordered per the code's dependencies.

It evaluates all available configuration files and recipe data (known as metadata), managing dynamic variable expansion, dependencies, and code generation. It keeps track of all tasks being processed in order to ensure completion, maximizing the use of processing resources to reduce build time and being predictable. The development of BitBake is centralized in the `bitbake-devel@lists.openembedded.org` mailing list, and its code can be found in the `bitbake` subdirectory of Poky.

OpenEmbedded-Core

The OpenEmbedded-Core metadata collection provides the engine of the Poky build tool. It is designed to provide the core features and to be as lean as possible. It provides support for seven different processor architectures (ARM, ARM64, x86, x86-64, PowerPC, MIPS, and MIPS64), supporting only boards to be emulated by QEMU.

The development is centralized in the `openembedded-core@lists.openembedded.org` mailing list and houses its metadata inside the `meta` subdirectory of Poky.

Metadata

The metadata which is composed of a mix of Python and Shell Script text files, provides a tremendously flexible system. Poky uses this to extend OpenEmbedded-Core and includes two different layers, which are another metadata subsets shown as follows:

- `meta-poky`: This layer provides the default and supported distributions, visual branding, and metadata tracking information (maintainers, upstream status, and so on)
- `meta-yocto-bsp`: Provides the **Board Support Package** (**BSP**) used as the reference for the Yocto Project development and **Quality Assurance** (**QA**) process

`Chapter 8`, *Developing with Yocto Projects,* explores the metadata in more detail and serves as a reference when we write our own recipes.

The alliance of the OpenEmbedded Project and the Yocto Project

The OpenEmbedded project was created around January 2003 when some core developers from the **OpenZaurus** project started to work with the new build system. The OpenEmbedded build system has been, since its beginning, a task scheduler inspired and based on the **Gentoo Portage** package system named BitBake. The project has grown its software collection and supported machine set at a fast pace.

As consequence of uncoordinated development, it was difficult to use OpenEmbedded in products that demand a more stable and polished code base, which is why Poky was born. Poky started as a subset of OpenEmbedded and had a more polished and stable code base across a limited set of architectures. Its reduced size allowed Poky to start to develop highlighting technologies, such as IDE plugins and QEMU integration, which are still being used today.

Around November 2010, the Yocto Project was announced by the Linux Foundation to continue this work under a Linux Foundation-sponsored project. The Yocto Project and OpenEmbedded Project consolidated their efforts on a core build system called OpenEmbedded-Core, using the best of both Poky and OpenEmbedded, thus emphasizing an increased use of additional components, metadata, and subsets.

Summary

This first chapter provided an overview of how the OpenEmbedded Project is related to the Yocto Project, the components which form Poky, and how it was created. In the next chapter, we will be introduced to the Poky workflow with steps to download, configure, and prepare the Poky build environment, and how to have the very first image built and running using QEMU.

2
Baking Our Poky-Based System

In this chapter we will understand the basic concepts involved in the Poky workflow. Let's get our hands dirty with the steps to download and configure, prepare the Poky build environment, and bake something usable. The steps covered here are commonly used for testing and development. They give us the whole experience of using Poky and a taste of its capabilities.

Configuring a host system

The process that we need to set up on our host system depends on the distribution we run on it. Poky has a set of supported Linux distributions, and if we are new to embedded Linux development, it is advisable to use one of the supported Linux distributions to avoid wasting time debugging build issues related to the host system support.

If you use the current release of one of following distributions, you should be good:

- Ubuntu
- Fedora
- CentOS
- Debian
- openSUSE

To confirm if your version is supported, it is advisable to check the official documentation online at `http://www.yoctoproject.org/docs/current/mega-manual/mega-manual.html#detailed-supported-distros`.

If your preferred distribution is not on the preceding list, it doesn't mean it is not possible to use Poky on it. However, it is unknown whether it will work, and we may get unexpected results.

The packages that need to be installed into the host system vary from one distribution to another. Throughout this book, you will find instructions for **Debian** and **Fedora**, our preferred distributions. You can find the instructions for all supported distributions in the *Yocto Project Reference Manual*.

Installing Poky on Debian

To install the necessary packages for a headless host system, run the following command:

```
$ sudo apt-get install gawk wget git-core diffstat unzip texinfo gcc-
multilib build-essential chrpath socat cpio python python3 python3-pip
python3-pexpect xz-utils debianutils iputils-ping
```

If our host system has graphics support, run the following command:

```
$ sudo apt-get install libsdl1.2-dev xterm
```

The preceding commands are also compatible with the Ubuntu distributions.

Installing Poky on Fedora

To install the needed packages for a headless host system, run the following command:

```
$ sudo dnf install gawk make wget tar bzip2 gzip python3 unzip perl patch
diffutils diffstat git cpp gcc gcc-c++ glibc-devel texinfo chrpath ccache
perl-Data-Dumper perl-Text-ParseWords perl-Thread-Queue perl-bignum socat
python3-pexpect findutils which file cpio python python3-pip xz which
```

If our host system has graphics support, run the following command:

```
$ sudo yum install SDL-devel xterm
```

Downloading the Poky source code

After we install the needed packages into our development host system, we need to get the Poky source code that can be downloaded with Git by using the following command:

```
$ git clone git://git.yoctoproject.org/poky -b rocko
```

Learn more about Git at http://git-scm.com.

After the download process is complete, we should have the following contents inside the poky directory:

```
⬤ – ☐  Content of Poky directory after download

$ ls -l
total 48
drwxrwxr-x  6 user user 4096 Out 22 12:36 bitbake
drwxrwxr-x 14 user user 4096 Out 22 12:36 documentation
-rw-rw-r--  1 user user  515 Out 22 12:36 LICENSE
drwxrwxr-x 19 user user 4096 Out 22 12:36 meta
drwxrwxr-x  5 user user 4096 Out 22 12:36 meta-poky
drwxrwxr-x  8 user user 4096 Out 22 12:36 meta-selftest
drwxrwxr-x  7 user user 4096 Out 22 12:36 meta-skeleton
drwxrwxr-x  8 user user 4096 Out 22 12:36 meta-yocto-bsp
-rwxrwxr-x  1 user user 1754 Out 22 12:36 oe-init-build-env
lrwxrwxrwx  1 user user   30 Out 22 12:36 README.hardware -> meta-yocto-bsp/README.hardware
-rw-rw-r--  1 user user 1173 Out 22 12:36 README.LSB
lrwxrwxrwx  1 user user   21 Out 22 12:36 README.poky -> meta-poky/README.poky
-rw-rw-r--  1 user user  529 Out 22 12:36 README.qemu
drwxrwxr-x  8 user user 4096 Out 22 12:36 scripts
$ █
```

The examples and code presented in this and the next chapters use the *Yocto Project Version 2.4*. The code name is Rocko, as the reference.

Preparing the build environment

Inside the `poky` directory, there is a script named `oe-init-build-env`, which should be used to set up the building environment. The script must be run as shown:

```
$ source oe-init-build-env [build-directory]
```

Here, `build-directory` is an optional parameter for the name of the directory where the environment is set; in case it is not given, it defaults to `build`. The `build-directory` is the place where we perform the builds.

It is very convenient to use different build directories. We can work on distinct projects in parallel or different experimental setups without affecting our other builds.

> Throughout the book, we will use build as the build directory. When we need to point to a file inside the build directory, we will adopt the same convention, for example, `build/conf/local.conf`.

Knowing the local.conf file

When we initialize a build environment, it creates a file called `build/conf/local.conf`, which is a powerful tool that can configure almost every aspect of the build process. We can set the machine we are building for, the toolchain host architecture to be used for a custom cross-toolchain, optimize options for maximum build time reduction, and so on. The comments inside the `build/conf/local.conf` file are a very good documentation and reference of possible variables, and their defaults. The minimal set of variables that we probably want to change from the default is the following:

```
MACHINE ??= "qemux86"
```

The `MACHINE` variable is where we determine the target machine we wish to build for. At the time of writing this book, Poky supports the following machines in its reference BSP:

- **beaglebone**: This is BeagleBone, that is the reference platform for 32-bit ARM
- **genericx86**: This is a generic support for 32-bit x86-based machines
- **genericx86-64**: This is a generic support for 64-bit x86-based machines
- **mpc8315e-rdb**: This is an NXP MPC8315 PowerPC reference platform
- **edgerouter**: This is EdgeRouter Lite, that is the reference platform for 64-bit MIPS

The machines are made available by a layer called `meta-yocto-bsp`. Besides these machines, OpenEmbedded-Core also provides support for the following:

- **qemuarm**: This is the QEMU ARM emulation
- **qemuarm64**: This is the QEMU ARM64 emulation
- **qemumips**: This is the QEMU MIPS emulation
- **qemumips64**: This is the QEMU MIPS64 emulation
- **qemuppc**: This is the QEMU PowerPC emulation
- **qemux86-64**: This is the QEMU x86-64 emulation
- **qemux86**: This is the QEMU x86 emulation

Other machines are supported through extra BSP layers and these are available from several vendors. The process of using an extra BSP layer is shown in `Chapter 10`, *Exploring External Layers*.

 The `local.conf` file is a very convenient way to override several default configurations over all the Yocto Project's tools. Essentially, we can change or set any variable, for example, add additional packages to an image file. Though it is convenient, it should be considered as a temporary change as the `build/conf/local.conf` file is not usually tracked by any source code management system.

There are several variables which can be set inside the `build/conf/local.conf` file. It is worth taking some time and reading the generated file comments to get a general idea.

Building a target image

Poky provides several predesigned image recipes that we can use to build our own binary image. We can check the list of available images by running the following command from the `poky` directory:

```
$ ls meta*/recipes*/images/*.bb
```

All the recipes provide images which are a set of unpacked and configured packages, generating a filesystem that we can use on a hardware or one of the supported QEMU machines.

Next, we can see the list of most commonly used images:

- **core-image-minimal**: This is a small image allowing a device to boot, and it is very useful for kernel and boot loader tests and development.

- **core-image-base**: This is a console-only image that fully supports the target device hardware.
- **core-image-weston**: This is an image that provides the Wayland protocol libraries and the reference Weston compositor.
- **core-image-x11**: This is a very basic X11 image with a terminal.
- **core-image-sato**: This is an image with Sato support and a mobile environment for mobile devices that use X11; it provides applications such as a terminal, editor, file manager, media player, and so forth.

The complete list would likely be outdated, so it's not included here. There are several different images supporting different features as Real Time, InitRAMFS, MTD (flash tools) and others. It is advisable to check the source code or the *Yocto Project Reference Manual* for the complete and updated list.

The process of building an image for a target is very simple. We must run the following command:

```
$ bitbake <recipe name>
```

We will use MACHINE = "qemuarm" in the following examples. It should be set in build/conf/local.conf accordingly.

For example, to build core-image-full-cmdline, run the following command:

```
$ bitbake core-image-full-cmdline
```

Running images in QEMU

As many projects have a small portion that is hardware dependent, the hardware emulation comes to speed up the development process by enabling a test run without involving any actual hardware.

Quick EMUlator (**QEMU**) is a free and open source software package that performs hardware virtualization. The QEMU-based machines allow test and development without real hardware. Currently, the ARM, ARM64, MIPS, MIPS64, PowerPC, and x86 and x86-64 emulations are supported.

The `runqemu` script enables and makes use of QEMU with the OpenEmbedded-Core supported machines easier. The way to run the script is as follows:

```
$ runqemu <machine> <zimage> <filesystem>
```

Here, `<machine>` is the machine/architecture to be used as `qemuarm`, `qemumips`, `qemuppc`, `qemux86`, or `qemux86-64`. Also, `<zimage>` is the path to a kernel (for example, `zimage-qemuarm.bin`). Finally, `<filesystem>` is the path to an `ext3` image (for example, `filesystem-qemuarm.ext3`) or an NFS directory. The parameters `<zimage>` and `<filesystem>` are optional.

So, for example, in case we run `runqemu qemuarm core-image-full-cmdline`, we can see something as shown in the following screenshot:

We can log in to the root account using an empty password. The system behaves as a regular system even being used inside the QEMU. The process to deploy an image in a real hardware varies depending on the type of storage used, bootloader, and so on. However, the process to generate the image is the same. We explore how to build and run an image in the BeagleBone Black, Raspberry Pi 3, and Wandboard machines in Chapter 14, *Booting Our Custom Embedded Linux*.

Summary

In this chapter we learned the steps needed to set up Poky and get our first image built. We ran that image using runqemu, which gave us a good overview of the available capabilities. In the next chapter, we will be introduced to Toaster, which provides a human friendly interface for BitBake, and we will use it to build an image and customize it further.

3
Using Toaster to Bake an Image

Now that we know how to build an image using BitBake within Poky, we will learn how to do the same using Toaster. We are going to focus on the simplest usage of Toaster and also mention what else Toaster can do so you know about its capabilities.

What is Toaster?

Toaster is a web interface that's used to configure and run builds. It communicates with the BitBake and Poky build system to manage and gather information about builds, packages, and images.

There are two ways of using Toaster:

- **Locally**: We can run Toaster as a local instance. This is suitable for single-user development, providing a graphic interface to the BitBake command lines and some build information.
- **Hosted**: This is suitable for multiple users. When Toaster is set up as a hosted instance, its components can be spread across several machines so the users' builds are run on the Toaster build servers.

In this chapter, we are going to use Toaster as a local instance. If you want to use it as a hosted instance, please look at the following website: http://www.yoctoproject.org/docs/current/toaster-manual/toaster-manual.html.

Bear in mind that every hosted service requires attention with its security. Think about this before using a hosted instance.

Installing Toaster

Toaster is written using the Python Django framework, so the easiest way of installing it is using Python's pip utility. We have already installed this when configuring our host machine in Chapter 2, *Baking Our Poky-Based System*, so we can install the rest of Toaster's requirements inside of Poky's directory:

```
$ pip3 install --user -r bitbake/toaster-requirements.txt
```

Starting Toaster

Once we have installed Toaster's requirements, we are ready to start its server. To do this, we should go to Poky's directory and run the following commands:

```
$ source oe-init-build-env
$ source toaster start
```

To access the Toaster web interface, open your favorite browser and enter http://127.0.0.1:8000.

By default, Toaster starts on port 8000. The webport parameter allows a different port to be used, for example, $ source toaster start webport=8400.

Next, we see the starting page of Toaster:

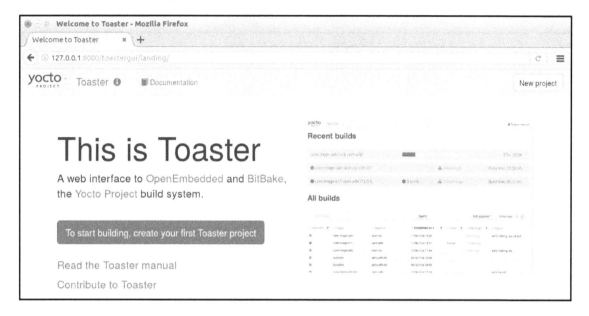

Building an image to QEMU

Following the same steps used in Chapter 2, *Baking Our Poky-Based System*, we are going to build an image to the QEMU ARM emulation.

The first step is to create the first project, which is a collection of configurations and builds that have already been performed.

As we don't have a project, we need to start one. Create a **Project name** and choose the target release, as shown in the following screenshot:

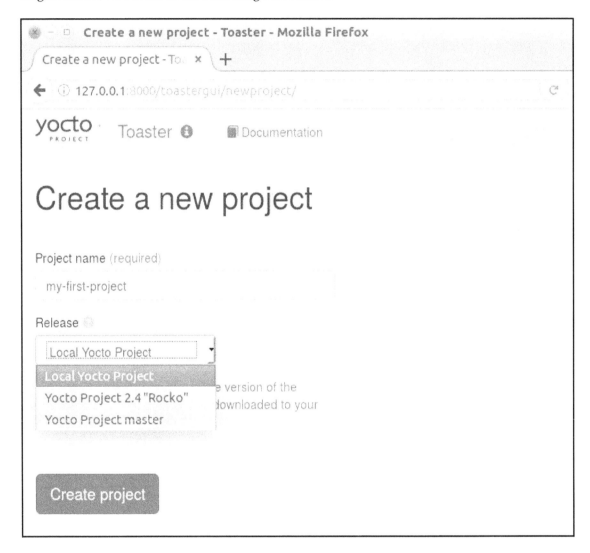

After creating `my-first-project`, we can see the main project screen, as shown in the following screenshot:

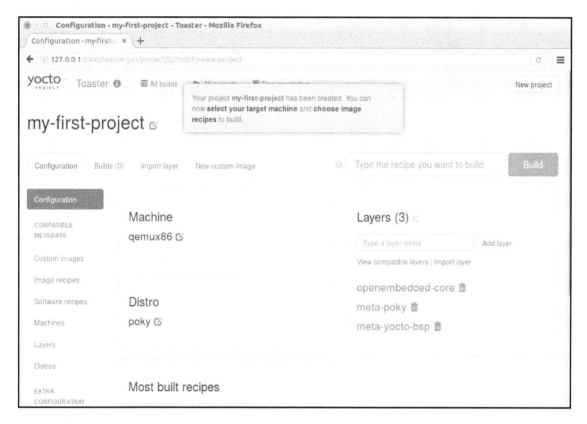

While on the **Configuration** tab, go to **Machine** and change it to `qemuarm`:

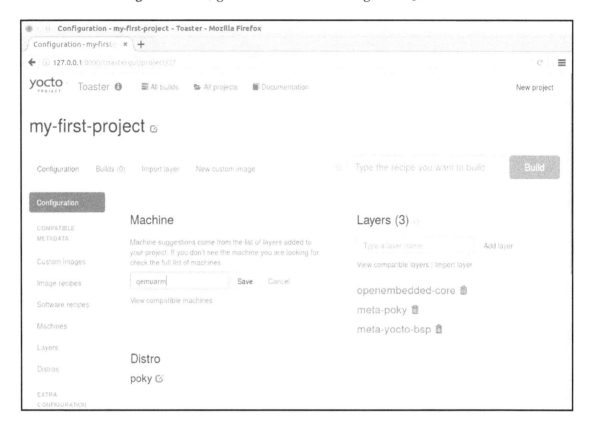

After that, click the **Image Recipes** tab to choose the image you want to build. In this example, as used in `Chapter 2`, *Baking Our Poky-Based System*, we can build `core-image-full-cmdline`:

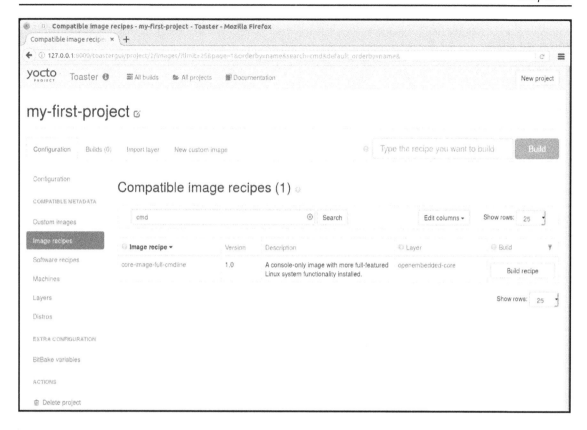

The following screenshot shows the build process:

The build process takes some time, but after that, we can see the built image along with some statistics:

We can also verify the generated set of files, as shown in the following screenshot:

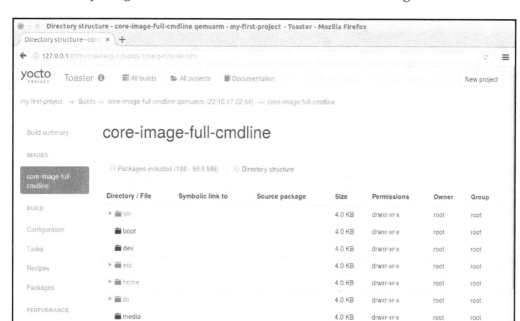

Toaster is a powerful tool. It can be used either on a local development machine or on a shared server to get a graphic representation of the build. Most tasks performed by BitBake can be achieved using Toaster as well.

Summary

In this chapter, we were introduced to Toaster and its basic features. We went through the process of installing and configuring Toaster, and we built and inspected an image.

In the next chapter, we are going to present some important BitBake concepts, and we believe these concepts are essential to really understand the Yocto Project as a whole. We will use BitBake and the command line for the rest of the book as they provide an internal view of all the concepts.

4
Grasping the BitBake Tool

We will now begin our journey of learning how the Yocto Project's engine works behind the scenes. As with every journey, communication is critical, so we need to learn the language used by the Yocto Project's tools and learn how to get the best out of these tools in order to accomplish our goals.

In the preceding chapters, we were introduced to the standard Yocto Project workflow for creating and emulating images. Now, in this chapter, we will explore the concept of metadata, see how recipes depend on each other, and how those recipes are used by Poky.

Besides the dependencies, there are other aspects that are important for every recipe. From downloading source code to generating images, there is a huge list of tasks, such as storing the source code in the directory used for the build; patching, configuring, compiling, installing, and generating the packages; and determining how the packages fit into the generated images.

Understanding the BitBake tool

The BitBake task scheduler started as a fork from Portage, which is the package management system used in the Gentoo distribution. However, the two projects have diverged a lot due to different usage focuses. The Yocto Project and the OpenEmbedded Project are the most well-known and intensive users of BitBake, which remains a separate and independent project with its own development cycle and mailing list (`bitbake-devel@lists.openembedded.org`).

As presented in `Chapter 1`, *Meeting the Yocto Project*, BitBake is a task scheduler that parses Python and the shell script mixed code. Based on the metadata, BitBake generates a large number of tasks that may have a complex dependency chain, so BitBake is responsible for ensuring those dependencies are met by maximizing the use of computational resources and running as many tasks as possible in parallel. BitBake can be understood as a tool similar to GNU Make in some respects.

In this chapter, we will cover the main aspects of BitBake. However, for more in-depth details about the tool, please refer to `https://www.yoctoproject.org/docs/current/bitbake-user-manual/bitbake-user-manual.html`.

Exploring metadata

The metadata used by BitBake can be classified into three major areas:

- Configuration (the `.conf` files)
- Classes (the `.bbclass` files)
- Recipes (the `.bb` and `.bbappend` files)

The configuration files define the global content, which is used to provide information and configure how the recipes will work. One common example of the configuration file is the machine file, which has a list of settings that describes the hardware.

The classes are used by the whole system and can be inherited by recipes according to their needs, or by default, and are used to define the system's behavior and provide the base methods. For example, `kernel.bbclass` helps to abstract common tasks related to building and packaging the Linux kernel independently of version or vendor changes.

The recipes and classes are written in a mix of Python and shell scripting code.

The classes and recipes describe the tasks to be run and provide the information needed to allow BitBake to generate the required task chain, as well as its dependencies information. The inheritance mechanism that permits a recipe to inherit one or more classes is used to reduce code duplication, improve accuracy, and make maintenance easier. A Linux kernel recipe example is `linux-yocto_4.12.bb`, which inherits a set of classes, including `kernel.bbclass`.

BitBake's most commonly used aspects across all types of metadata (`.conf`, `.bb`, and `.bbclass`) are shown in the following sections.

The metadata grammar and syntax are detailed in `Chapter 7`, *Diving into BitBake Metadata*.

Parsing metadata

As previously mentioned, there are three metadata groups—configuration, class, and recipe.

The first parsed metadata in BitBake is configuration metadata, identified by the `.conf` file extension. This metadata is global, and therefore affects all recipes and tasks that are executed.

BitBake first searches the current working directory for the `build/conf/bblayers.conf` configuration file, which is expected to contain a `BBLAYERS` variable that is a space-delimited list of layer directories. For each directory in this list, a `conf/layer.conf` file is searched for and parsed to add the recipes, classes, and configurations contained within that particular layer. `LAYERDIR` is set to the directory where the layer was found during this process and also adds this layer to the `BBPATH` list, which points to the set of directories with recipes, classes, and configurations.

The order of the listed layers in the `BBLAYERS` variable is followed by BitBake when parsing the metadata. If your layer needs to be parsed first, be sure to have it listed in the right place in `BBLAYERS`.

After parsing all the layers in use, BitBake starts to parse the metadata. It first loads `meta/conf/bitbake.conf` from one of the paths included in the `BBPATH` list. Similar to many other BitBake configuration files, the `meta/conf/bitbake.conf` file uses `include` directives to pull in other metadata, such as architecture-specific metadata, machine configuration files, and the `build/conf/local.conf` file. One important restriction of BitBake configuration files (`.conf`) is that only variable definitions and `include` directives are allowed.

BitBake's classes (`.bbclass`), as mentioned earlier, are a rudimentary inheritance mechanism. They are parsed when an `inherit` directive is encountered, and they are located in `classes/`, relative to the directories in `BBPATH`.

A BitBake recipe (.bb) is a logical unit of tasks to be executed. Normally, this is a package built to obey the inter-recipe dependencies. The files themselves are found via the BBFILES variable, which is set to a space-separated list of the .bb files and handles wildcards.

Dependencies

In order to accomplish the dependency, the recipes must declare what dependencies they need to have available during the build process. BitBake ensures that the build-time dependencies are satisfied before starting to build the recipe. This is easier to understand if we think about an application that uses a library. So, this library must be built and its headers must be made available for use before the application itself can be built. The DEPENDS variable is used in a recipe to inform BitBake about the build-time dependency and we should list another recipe.

When an application depends on something to run, it is called a runtime dependency. This is common for shared data among applications (for example, icons) that is used only when running the application or when an application calls another application during its execution that is not used during its build process. The runtime dependencies can be expressed using the RDEPENDS variable in a recipe. However, as those are meant to express runtime requirements, we should list package names here. In Chapter 6, *Assimilating Packaging Support*, we explain more how packaging happens.

Knowing the recipe dependencies chain, BitBake can sort all the recipes for the build in a feasible order. This enables BitBake to organize tasks in the following ways:

- Recipes that do not have a dependency relation are built in parallel
- Dependent recipes are built in a serial order, sorted in the way the dependencies are satisfied.

Every recipe included in the runtime dependencies is put in the build list. This sounds obvious, but even though they are not used during the build, they are included because they need to be ready for use so that the resulting binary packages are installable.

Preferring and providing recipes

The dependency relation between recipes is essential to BitBake and Poky. It is defined inside each recipe file, with a variable that describes on what a recipe depends (DEPENDS) and what a recipe provides to the system (PROVIDES). These two variables together build the dependency graph used by BitBake during dependency resolution.

So, if a recipe called foo_1.0.bb depends on bar, BitBake lists all recipes providing bar. The bar dependency can be satisfied by the following:

- A recipe with the bar_<version>.bb format, because every recipe provides itself
- A recipe where the PROVIDES variable includes bar

A dependency can be satisfied by several recipes (for example, if two or more recipes have PROVIDES += "bar"). In this case, we must inform BitBake which specific provider to use.

The virtual/kernel provider is a clear example where this mechanism is used. The virtual/ namespace is the convention adopted when we have a set of commonly overridden providers.

All recipes that require the kernel to build can add virtual/kernel to the dependency list (DEPENDS), and BitBake makes sure to satisfy the dependency. When we have more than one recipe with an alternative provider, we must choose one to be used, for example, PREFERRED_PROVIDER_virtual/kernel = "linux-mymachine".

The virtual/kernel provider is commonly set in the machine definition file, as it may vary from one machine to another. We will see how to create a machine definition file in Chapter 11, *;Creating Custom Layers*.

 When BitBake cannot satisfy a dependency due to a missing provider, an error is raised.

In the same system, two recipes cannot use different providers for the same dependency. When BitBake has two providers with different versions, it uses the highest version by default. We can force BitBake to use a different version by using `PREFERRED_VERSION`. This is commonly found in BSPs, such as bootloaders, where vendors may use specific versions for a board.

When we have a development or an unreliable version of a recipe, and we do not want it to be used by default, we can use `DEFAULT_PREFERENCE = "-1"` in the recipe file. So, even if the version is higher, it is not taken without it being explicitly set (using `PREFERRED_VERSION`).

Fetching the source code

When the Poky source code is downloaded, what is actually copied is the metadata and the BitBake tool. Additional source code is fetched on demand. One of the main features supported by BitBake is source code fetching.

This support has been designed to be as modular and as flexible as possible. Every Linux-based system includes the Linux kernel and several other utilities that form the root filesystem, such as OpenSSH or a Linux kernel.

The OpenSSH source code is available from its upstream website as a `tar.gz` file hosted on an HTTP server, while the Linux kernel release is usually hosted on a Git repository, and those two different source codes can easily be fetched by BitBake.

BitBake offers support for many different fetcher modules that allow the retrieval of tarball files and a number of other protocols, such as Git, Subversion, Bazaar, OSC, HTTP, HTTPS, FTP, CVS, Mercurial, Perforce, and SSH.

The mechanism used by BitBake to fetch the source code is internally called as fetcher backends that are configurable to align the user's requirements and optimize fetching the source code .

Remote file downloads

BitBake supports several methods for remote file downloads. The most commonly used are `http://`, `https://`, and `git://`. We won't cover the internal details of how BitBake handles remote file downloads and will instead focus on its visible effects.

When BitBake executes the `do_fetch` task in a recipe, it checks the `SRC_URI` contents. If we look at, for example, the `libmpc` recipe (available at `meta/recipes-support/libmpc/libmpc_1.0.3.bb`), the processed variables are the following:

```
SRC_URI = "http://www.multiprecision.org/mpc/download/mpc-${PV}.tar.gz"
SRC_URI[md5sum] = "d6a1d5f8ddea3abd2cc3e98f58352d26"
SRC_URI[sha256sum] =
"617decc6ea09889fb08ede330917a00b16809b8db88c29c31bfbb49cbf88ecc3"
```

BitBake expands the `PV` variable to the package version (`1.0.3` in this example), downloads the file from `http://www.multiprecision.org/mpc/download/mpc-1.0.3.tar.gz`, and then saves it onto the download storage directory, which is defined by `DL_DIR` variable.

After the download is complete, BitBake compares the `md5sum` and `sha256sum` values of the downloaded file with the values from the recipe, and if both values match, it creates a `${DL_DIR}/mpc-1.0.3.tar.gz.done` file to mark the file as successfully downloaded and checked. This way, when BitBake looks for the file next time, it knows that it can safely be reused and it skips the file's checksum verification. This process happens for every remote file that BitBake downloads.

By default, the `DL_DIR` variable points to `build/downloads`. You can override this using the `build/conf/local.conf` file like this: `DL_DIR = "/my/download-cache"`. This makes it easy to share the same download cache among several different build directories, thus saving time and bandwidth.

Git repositories

One of the most commonly used source control management systems in use is Git. BitBake has a solid support for Git, and the Git backend is used when the `do_fetch` task is run and finds a `git://` URL at the `SRC_URI` variable.

The default way for BitBake's Git backend to handle the repositories is to clone the repository into `${DL_DIR}/git2/<git URL>`. For example, check the following quote from the `linux-firmware_git.bb` recipe found in `meta/recipes-kernel/linux-firmware/linux-firmware_git.bb` inside Poky:

```
SRCREV = "a61ac5cf8374edbfe692d12f805a1b194f7fead2"
...
SRC_URI = "git://git.kernel.org/pub/scm/linux/kernel/git/firmware/linux-firmware.git"
```

Here, the `linux-firmware.git` repository is cloned into `${DL_DIR}/git2/git.kernel.org.pub.scm.linux.kernel.git.firmware.linux-firmware.git`.

This directory name is chosen to avoid conflicts between other possible Git repositories with the same project name. The `SRCREV` variable is used by the `do_fetch` task to ensure the repository has the required Git revision and forces an update in case it does not; it's used by the `do_unpack` task to set up the working directory in the required source revision.

When the `SRCREV` variable points to a hash that's not available in the master branch, we need to use the `branch=<branch name>` parameter as follows: `SRC_URI = "git://myserver/myrepo.git;branch=mybranch"`. In cases when the hash used points to a tag that is not available on a branch, we need to use the `nobranch=1` option as follows: `SRC_URI = "git://myserver/myrepo.git;nobranch=1"`.

The remote file and the Git repository are the most commonly used fetch backends of BitBake. The other source code management support systems vary in their implementations, but the general ideas and concepts are the same.

Optimizing the source code download

To improve the robustness of source code download, Poky provides a mirror mechanism that can be configured in order to do the following:

- Provide a centrally preferred server for download
- Provide fallback servers

In order to provide this robust download mechanism, BitBake follows some steps. During the build, the first BitBake step is to search for the source code within the local download directory (specified by `DL_DIR`). In case of failure, the next step is to try locations defined by the `PREMIRRORS` variable. In a recurrent case of failure, it searches the locations specified in the `MIRRORS` variable.

The following section explains the PREMIRRORS and MIRRORS variables:

- PREMIRRORS: The second step in the download mechanism performed by BitBake is controlled by the PREMIRRORS variable. For example, the Poky distribution sets it as follows:

```
PREMIRRORS ??= "\
bzr://.*/.* http://downloads.yoctoproject.org/mirror/sources/ \n \
cvs://.*/.* http://downloads.yoctoproject.org/mirror/sources/ \n \
git://.*/.* http://downloads.yoctoproject.org/mirror/sources/ \n \
gitsm://.*/. *http://downloads.yoctoproject.org/mirror/sources/ \n
\
hg://.*/.* http://downloads.yoctoproject.org/mirror/sources/ \n \
osc://.*/.* http://downloads.yoctoproject.org/mirror/sources/ \n \
p4://.*/.* http://downloads.yoctoproject.org/mirror/sources/ \n \
svn://.*/.* http://downloads.yoctoproject.org/mirror/sources/ \n"
```

- The preceding code prepends the PREMIRRORS variable to change and instruct the build system to intercept any Git, FTP, HTTP, and HTTPS requests, and it redirects them to the http://www.yoctoproject.org/sources/ source's mirror.
- In case the desired component is not available in the source mirror, BitBake falls back to the MIRRORS variable.

- MIRRORS: The MIRRORS variable provides a set of alternative URL addresses for some servers where the source component may be found. BitBake tries one after another, and if all available mirrors fail, it raises an error:

```
MIRRORS =+ "\
ftp://.*/.*        http://downloads.yoctoproject.org/mirror/sources/
\n \
http://.*/.*       http://downloads.yoctoproject.org/mirror/sources/
\n \
https://.*/.*      http://downloads.yoctoproject.org/mirror/sources/
\n"
```

We can take advantage of this download mechanism to save download time by providing a local pull directory or a local network server by adding the following code to build/conf/local.conf:

```
SOURCE_MIRROR_URL ?= "file:///home/you/your-download-dir/"
INHERIT += "own-mirrors"
```

Here, SOURCE_MIRROR_URL can point to a local directory or to any server URL with the supported fetcher backend.

 If the goal is to have a shareable download cache, it is advisable to enable the tarball generation for the SCM backends (for example, Git) in the download folder with BB_GENERATE_MIRROR_TARBALLS = "1" in build/conf/local.conf.

Disabling network access

Sometimes, we need to ensure that we don't connect to the internet during the build process. There are several valid reasons for this, such as the following:

- **Policy**: Our company does not allow external sources to be included in a product without a proper legal validation and review.
- **Network cost**: When we are on the road using mobile broadband, the cost of data may be too high because the data to download may be large.
- **Download and build decoupling:** This setup is commonly used in constant integration environments so that a build job can be used to download all the required source code while the build workers have the internet access disabled. This ensures no source is downloaded in duplication and that we have all required source code cached.
- **Lack of network access**: Sometimes, we do not have access to a network

In order to disable the network connection, we need to add the following code in the build/conf/local.conf file:

```
BB_NO_NETWORK = "1"
```

Understanding BitBake's tasks

BitBake uses execution units, which are in essence a set of clustered instructions that run in sequence. These units are known as **tasks**. There are many tasks being scheduled, executed, and checked by BitBake during every recipe's build, provided by classes to form the framework that we use to build a recipe. It is important to understand some of these as we often use, extend, implement, or replace them ourselves when writing a recipe.

Run the following command:

```
$ bitbake <recipe>
```

BitBake runs a set of scheduled tasks. When we wish to run a specific task, we can use the following command:

```
$ bitbake <recipe> -c <task>
```

To list the tasks defined for a recipe, we can use the following command:

```
$ bitbake <recipe> -c listtasks
```

We will briefly describe each of these here:

- do_fetch: The first step when building a recipe is fetching the required source. This is done using the fetching backends feature we discussed previously in this chapter. It is important to point out that fetching a source or a file does not mean it is a remote source. In fact, every file needed during the recipe build must be fetched so that it is made available in the WORKDIR directory. We will learn more about the build directory and its contents in Chapter 5, *Detailing the Temporary Build Directory*. All downloaded content is stored in the download folder (the DL_DIR variable), so all external source code is cached to avoid downloading it every time we need the same source.

- do_unpack: The natural subsequent task after the do_fetch task is do_unpack. This is responsible for unpacking source code or checking out the requested revision or branch in case the referenced source uses an SCM system.

- do_patch: Once the source code has been properly unpacked, BitBake initiates the process of adapting the source code. This is done by the do_patch task. Every file fetched by do_fetch, with the .patch extension, is assumed to be a patch to be applied. This task applies the list of patches needed.

- do_configure, do_compile, and do_install: The do_configure, do_compile, and do_install tasks are performed in this order. Some recipes may omit one task or another. It is important to note that the environment variables defined in the tasks are different from one task to another. The tasks vary a lot from one recipe to another. Poky provides a rich collection of predefined tasks in the classes, which ought to be used when possible. For example, when the autotools class is inherited by a recipe, it provides a known implementation of the do_configure, do_compile, and do_install tasks.

- do_package: The do_package task splits the files installed by the recipe into logical components such as debugging symbols, documentation, and libraries. The do_package task ensures that files are split up and packaged correctly. We will cover the packaging details in more depth in Chapter 6, *Assimilating Package Support*.

Extending tasks

When the task content does not satisfy our requirements, we replace it (providing our own implementation) or append it. As we will learn more extensively when learning about the BitBake metadata syntax in Chapter 7, *Diving into BitBake Metadata*, the _append and _prepend operators can be used to extend a task with extra content. The new content is concatenated in the original task. For example, to extend a do_install task, we can use the following code:

```
do_install_append() {
# Do my commands
}
```

The mechanisms we can use to extend existing recipes are covered in Chapter 12, *Customizing Existing Recipes*.

Generating a root filesystem image

One of the most common uses of Poky is the rootfs image generation. The rootfs image should be seen as a ready-to-use root filesystem for a target. The image can be made up of one or more filesystems and may include other artifacts to be available during its generation, such as the Linux kernel, device tree, and bootloader binaries. The process of generating the image is composed of several steps, and its most common usages are as follows:

1. Generate the rootfs directory.
2. Create the required files.
3. Wrap the final filesystem according to the specific requirements (it may be a disk file with several partitions and contents).
4. Finally, compress it, if applicable.

All these steps are performed by subtasks of do_rootfs.

rootfs is basically a directory with the desired packages installed (package generation is covered in Chapter 6, *Assimilating Packaging Support*), with the required tweaks applied just afterward. The tweaks make minor adjustments to the rootfs contents; for example, when building a development image, rootfs is adjusted to allow us to log in as root without a password.

The list of packages to be installed into `rootfs` is defined by a union of packages listed by `IMAGE_INSTALL` and the packages included by `IMAGE_FEATURES`; the image customization is detailed in Chapter 11, *Creating Custom Layers*. Each image feature can include extra packages for installation, for example, `dev-pkgs`, which installs development libraries and headers of all packages listed to be installed in `rootfs`.

The list of packages to be installed is now filtered by the `PACKAGE_EXCLUDE` variable, which lists the packages that should not be installed. The packages listed in `PACKAGE_EXCLUDE` are only excluded from the list of packages to be explicitly installed.

> Packages listed in `PACKAGE_EXCLUDE` are installed into `rootfs` if they are needed to satisfy a runtime dependency.

Having the final set of packages to install, the `do_rootfs` task can initiate the process of unpacking and configuring each package, and its required dependencies, into the `rootfs` directory. This is done using a package backend's (DEB, IPK, or RPM) specific set of subtasks as it actually uses the package management system using a local package feed to do this step. The package feed is explained in Chapter 6, *Assimilating Packaging Support*.

With the `rootfs` contents unpacked, the post installation scripts of the referred packages must run to avoid the penalty of running them during first boot. Some scripts may need to be run in the target to succeed, and there is no problem with that, except when we use the `read-only-rootfs` image feature. The post-installation script and the other variants of it are covered in Chapter 6, *Assimilating Packaging Support*.

> All the post-installation scripts must be successful with a read-only `rootfs` directory.

The `rootfs` optimization is then executed. A `prelink` process optimizes the dynamic linking of shared libraries to reduce the startup time of the executables; the `mklibs` process optimizes the size of the libraries by removing the unused symbols. Now, the directory is ready to generate the filesystem. `IMAGE_FSTYPES` lists the filesystem to be generated, for example, `EXT4` or `UBIFS`.

After `do_rootfs` has completely finished, the generated image file is placed in `build/tmp/deploy/image/<machine>/`. The process of creating our image and the possible values for `IMAGE_FEATURES` and `IMAGE_FSTYPES` are described in Chapter 11, *Creating Custom Layers*.

Summary

In this chapter, we learned about the concept of metadata, how recipes depend on each other, and how Poky deals with dependencies. We got a better view of the tasks being managed by BitBake to download all the required source code and used it to build and generate packages, and saw how these packages fit into generated images.

In the next chapter, we will see the contents of the build directory after complete image generation and learn how BitBake uses it in the baking process, including the contents of the temporary build directory and its generated files.

5
Detailing the Temporary Build Directory

In this chapter, we will understand the contents of the temporary build directory after a complete image generation and see how BitBake uses it in the baking process. We will learn how some of these directories can assist our understanding when things do not work as expected, providing a valuable source of information.

Detailing the build directory

The build directory is a central information and artifact source for every Poky user. Its main directories are the following:

- `conf`: This has the configuration files we use to control Poky and BitBake. The first use of this directory was in Chapter 2, *Baking Our Poky-Based System*. It stores configuration files such as `build/conf/local.conf` and `build/conf/bblayers.conf`.
- `downloads`: This stores all the downloaded artifacts. It can be seen as the download cache and has been detailed in Chapter 4, *Grasping the BitBake Tool*.
- `sstate-cache`: This has the packaged data snapshots. It is a cache mainly used to speed up the build process. This folder is detailed in Chapter 6, *Assimilating Packaging Support*.
- `tmp`: This is the temporary build directory and the main focus of this chapter.

Constructing the build directory

Poky's inputs and outputs were already detailed at a high level of abstract in the previous chapters. We already know that BitBake uses metadata to generate different types of artifacts, including images. Besides the generated artifacts, BitBake creates much more content during this process, which may be used in several ways, dependent upon our goals.

During the build process, BitBake performs several tasks and continuously modifies the build directory. We can understand it better following the usual BitBake flow, as follows:

- **Fetching**: The first action realized by BitBake is to download the source code. This step may modify the build directory as it tries to use the cached downloaded copy of the source code, or performs the download and stores it inside the `build/download` directory.

- **Source preparation**: After fetching the source code is complete, it must be prepared for use. This may involve, for example, the unpacking of a tarball or a clone of a local cached Git directory (from the download cache). The source code is prepared in the `build/tmp/work` directory. When the source code is ready, the required modifications are applied (for example, applying necessary patches).

- **Configuration and building**: With the ready-to-use source code, the building process starts. It involves the configuration of build options (for example, `./configure`) and building (for example, `make`).

- **Installing**: The built artifacts are then installed (for example, `make install`) in a proper directory under `build/tmp/work/<...>/image`.

- **Wrapping the sysroot**: The libraries, headers, and other files that need to be shared for cross-compilation are copied (and sometimes modified) in `build/tmp/work/<...>/recipe-sysroot` and `build/tmp/work/<...>/recipe-sysroot-native`.

- **Creating the packages**: The packages are generated using the installed contents, potentially splitting this content across multiple packages, which can be provided in different formats, for example, `.rpm` or `.ipk`.

 Until the *Yocto Project 2.2 (Morty)* release, we used a global sysroot directory for each machine and architecture but since the *Yocto Project 2.3 (Pyro)* release, we have a `sysroot` for each recipe, which boosts the determinism of the build system.

Exploring the temporary build directory

It is critical to understand the temporary build directory (build/tmp). The temporary build directory is created just after the build starts, and it's especially important for helping us to identify why something didn't behave as expected.

The contents of the build/tmp directory are shown in the following figure:

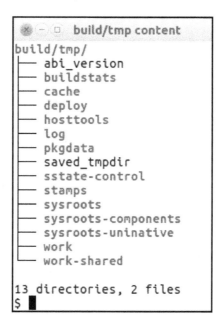

The most important directories found within it are the following:

- deploy: This contains the build products such as images, binary packages, and SDKs
- sysroots: This contains the shared libraries, headers, and utilities that are used in the process of building recipes
- work: This contains the working source code, a task's configuration, execution logs, and the contents of generated packages

Understanding the work directory

The `build/tmp/work` directory is organized by architecture. For example, when working with the machine `qemuarm`, we have the following four directories:

- `all-poky-linux`
- `armv5te-poky-linux-gnueabi`
- `qemuarm-poky-linux-gnueabi`
- `x86_64-linux`

The directories found here and their contents are architecture and machine dependent. We shouldn't take this as a final list, only as an illustration. The `x86_64-linux` directory is used to build the host sysroot content, which is detailed in the next section. The `all-poky-linux` directory holds the working build directories for the packages that are architecture agnostic. This fragmented structure is necessary to allow the building of multiple machines and architectures within one build directory, without conflicting with each other.

The target machine we use is `qemuarm`. This machine is an emulation of the **ARM Versatile Platform Baseboard** with the ARM926EJ-S CPU emulation that supports the ARMv5TE instructions. Poky treats `qemuarm` as a type of ARMv5TE because some hardware features may not be available on one device or another, even when they are supported by the CPU. Machine-specific recipes are built in the machine directory (`qemuarm-poky-linux-gnueabi` in this case) while the architecture-specific packages are built in the architecture-specific directory (`armv5te-poky-linux-gnueabi` in this case).

The `build/tmp/work` directory is very useful when checking for misbehavior or building failures. Its contents are stored in sub-directories following this pattern:

```
<arch>/<recipe name>/<software version>
```

Some of the directories under this tree are:

- `<sources>`: This is an extracted source code of the software to be built. This directory is pointed to the `WORKDIR` variable.
- `image`: This contains the files installed by the recipe (pointed to `D` variable).
- `packages`: The extracted contents of packages are stored here.
- `packages-split`: The contents of packages, extracted and split, are stored here. This has a sub-directory for each package.
- `temp`: This stores BitBake's task code and execution logs.

The most commonly checked sub-directories are under the `sysroot` directory, which provides the artifacts used during cross-compilation as compilers, utilities, and libraries for the host and target; they are also checked under the `build/tmp/work` directory, which holds the working build directory. These directories provide valuable information for debugging.

> In order to reduce disk usage, we can automatically remove the `work` directory after each recipe compilation cycle, adding `INHERIT +=` `"rm_work"` in the `build/conf/local.conf` file.

The structure of the `work` directory is the same for all architectures. For every recipe, a directory with the recipe name is created. Taking the machine-specific work directory and using the `sysvinit-inittab` recipe as an example, we see the following:

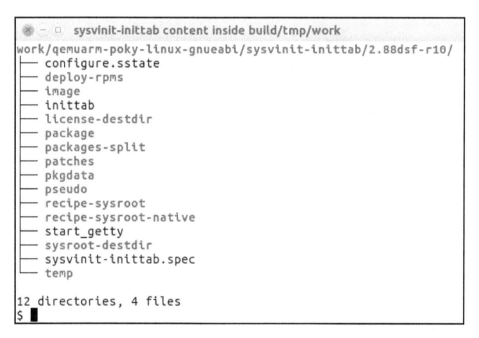

```
⊗ − □   sysvinit-inittab content inside build/tmp/work
work/qemuarm-poky-linux-gnueabi/sysvinit-inittab/2.88dsf-r10/
├── configure.sstate
├── deploy-rpms
├── image
├── inittab
├── license-destdir
├── package
├── packages-split
├── patches
├── pkgdata
├── pseudo
├── recipe-sysroot
├── recipe-sysroot-native
├── start_getty
├── sysroot-destdir
├── sysvinit-inittab.spec
└── temp

12 directories, 4 files
$ ▮
```

The `sysvinit-inittab` recipe is a good example, which even without a machine-specific object code is a machine-specific one. It contains the `inittab` file that defines, among other things, the serial console devices to spawn the login process, and this varies from machine to machine as the UART device depends on the machine schematic layout.

 The directories shown in the preceding figure that are not detailed here are used by the build system. You should not need to work with them, except if you are working on build tool development.

The `work` directory is very useful for debugging purposes; we cover this in Chapter 9, *Debugging with the Yocto Project*.

Understanding the sysroot directories

Traditionally, the Yocto Project's `sysroot` directory was shared among all the recipes and the build system environment, but this has a number of shortcomings as this macro environment has all the dependencies of all recipes previously built, and those libraries and utilities may influence other recipes. Since *Yocto Project 2.4 (Rocko)*, the sysroot structure has been improved to use a recipe-specific sysroot. The content of the sysroot directories are shown in the following figure:

```
⊗ – □  sysroots contents
$ tree -L 1 tmp/work/armv5e-poky-linux-gnueabi/procps/3.3.12-r0/recipe-sysroot*
tmp/work/armv5e-poky-linux-gnueabi/procps/3.3.12-r0/recipe-sysroot
├── lib
├── sysroot-providers
└── usr
tmp/work/armv5e-poky-linux-gnueabi/procps/3.3.12-r0/recipe-sysroot-native
├── bin
├── etc
├── installeddeps
├── lib
├── sbin
├── sysroot-providers
├── usr
└── var

11 directories, 0 files
$ tree -L 1 tmp/work/armv5e-poky-linux-gnueabi/procps/3.3.12-r0/recipe-sysroot/sysroot-providers/
tmp/work/armv5e-poky-linux-gnueabi/procps/3.3.12-r0/recipe-sysroot/sysroot-providers/
├── gcc-runtime
├── glibc
├── libgcc
├── libtool-cross
├── linux-libc-headers
├── ncurses
├── opkg-utils
├── virtual_arm-poky-linux-gnueabi-compilerlibs
├── virtual_arm-poky-linux-gnueabi-libc-for-gcc
├── virtual_libc
└── virtual_libiconv

0 directories, 11 files
$ tree -L 1 tmp/work/armv5e-poky-linux-gnueabi/procps/3.3.12-r0/recipe-sysroot-native/sysroot-providers/
tmp/work/armv5e-poky-linux-gnueabi/procps/3.3.12-r0/recipe-sysroot-native/sysroot-providers/
├── attr-native
├── autoconf-native
├── automake-native
├── binutils-cross-arm
├── bison-native
├── bzip2-native
├── bzip2-replacement-native
├── cryptodev-linux-native
├── db-native
├── dbus-native
```

After we build the `procps`, version 3.3.12, recipe, we get two sets of `sysroot` directories, as shown in the previous screenshot. The directories are `recipes-sysroot-native` and `recipes-sysroot`, and inside each sysroot set, there is a sub-directory called `sysroot-provides`. This directory lists the packages installed on each `sysroot`.

`recipe-sysroot-native` includes the build dependencies used in the host system during the build process. It is critical to the cross-compilation process because it encompasses the compiler, linker, build script tools, and more, while in the `recipe-sysroot` we have the libraries and headers used in the target code; in our example, we used qemuarm.

One common mistake to avoid when designing a library recipe is not getting its contents installed properly (the headers, static, and shared libraries) into the directory pointed to the D variable so that Poky can, most of the time, make the right installation of the files needed in sysroot. When we see a missing header or a link failure, we must double-check if our sysroot (target and host) contents are correct.

Summary

In this chapter, we explored the contents of the temporary build directory after a complete image generation and saw how BitBake uses it during the baking process. We then learned how to use these directories for debugging.

In the next chapter, we will get a better understanding of how packaging is done in Poky, how to use package feeds and the PR service, and how they may help in our product maintenance.

6
Assimilating Packaging Support

This chapter presents the key concepts for understanding the aspects of Poky and BitBake related to packaging. We will learn about the supported binary package formats, shared state cache, package versioning components, how to set up and use binary **package feeds** to support our development process, and more.

Using supported package formats

Packages are critical to Poky as they enable the build system to produce different types of artifacts, such as images and toolchains.

A recipe may generate one or more packages as a result of it being executed by BitBake. On the other hand, images and toolchains are made of several packages that are unpacked and configured to accomplish the intended goal. The generated result is wrapped in such a way that it can be installed into one or more images, or it can be deployed for later use.

List of supported package formats

Currently, BitBake supports four different package formats:

- **RPM**: Originally named **Red Hat Package Manager** (RPM), but now known as the RPM package format since its adoption by several other Linux distributions, it is used by popular Linux distributions such as SuSE, OpenSuSE, Red Hat, Fedora, and CentOS, among others.
- **DEB**: The **Debian Package Manager** is used by Debian and several other Debian-based distributions; the most widely known among them are Ubuntu Linux and Linux Mint.

- **IPK**: The **Itsy Package Management System** was a lightweight package management system designed for embedded devices that resembled Debian's package format. The initial project was discontinued, and several of the embedded build systems and distributions that used it were moved to the `Opkg` `fork` made by **OpenMoko**; it is also used by the *OpenWRT* project. Currently, OpenEmbedded-Core, and as a consequence Poky, use the Opkg package manager to support the IPK format.
- **TAR**: This is derived from the tape archive `.tar`, and it is a widely used tarball file type used to group several files into just a single file.

Choosing a package format

Support for formats is provided using a set of classes (`package_rpm`, `package_deb`, and `package_ipk`). We can select one or more formats using the `PACKAGE_CLASSES` variable, as shown in the following example:

```
PACKAGE_CLASSES ?= "package_rpm package_deb package_ipk"
```

This can be done, for example, in the `build/conf/local.conf` file. Using the `PACKAGE_CLASSES` variable, we can generate the packages in one or more formats.

Images are created from the first package format found in `PACKAGE_CLASSES`.

Poky defaults to the `RPM` package format, which uses the **DNF** package manager. However, the format choice depends on several aspects, including package format-specific features, memory and resource usage, and so on. Another aspect is habit; for example, OpenEmbedded-Core users often feel more comfortable using `IPK` and `opkg` as the package manager as it is OpenEmbedded-Core's default and offers a smaller footprint in memory and resource usage. On the other hand, people used to Debian-based systems may prefer to use the `APT` and `DEB` package formats for their products.

Running code during package installation

Packages can use scripts as part of their installation and removal process. The included scripts are defined as follows:

- preinst: This executes before the package is unpacked. Services should be stopped during the execution of preinst to permit installation or upgrading.
- postinst: This typically completes any required configuration of the package after it has been unpacked. Many postinst scripts then execute any command necessary to start or restart a service once a new package has been installed or upgraded.
- prerm: This usually stops any daemon that is associated with a package. It is executed before the removal of files associated with the package.
- postrm: This commonly modifies links or other files created by the package.

The scripts are supposed to be run after the package installation (postinst) is run during the root filesystem creation. If the script returns a success value, the package is marked as installed. If the script execution returns an error, the package is marked as unpacked. All packages marked as unpacked have their scripts executed again immediately in the first boot of the image.

In order to add a postinst script, we can use the following code as an example:

```
pkg_postinst_${PN} () {
#!/bin/sh -e
# Insert commands above
}
```

Instead of using the package name itself, we can use the PN variable, which automatically expands the package name of the recipe.

To delay script execution, so it runs on the target device itself, we use the following structure in the post-installation script:

```
pkg_postinst_${PN} () {
#!/bin/sh -e
if [ -n "$D" ]; then
    # Insert commands here
else
    exit 1
fi
}
```

In the previous example, we can see how the execution of the script is delayed. If the $D variable has a value, the script returns an error and the package is set as unpacked. It means that any command inserted in the conditional if section is executed only if the $D variable is unset.

We can also skip postscript execution, at rootfs creation time, for example, to avoid trying to start a daemon at that time, but yet ensure that it is properly started when being upgraded in the device. Here is one example:

```
pkg_postinst_${PN} () {
#!/bin/sh -e
if [ -n "$D" ]; then
    exit 0
fi
# Insert commands here to restart
}
```

When we generate an image with read-only-rootfs in IMAGE_FEATURES, all post-installation scripts must succeed. If any script returns an error and the package is set as unpacked only, forcing the script to be run after the root filesystem is created, the do_rootfs task fails. This check during build time ensures that we identify the problem while building the image rather than during the initial boot operation in the target device due to the impossibility of writing to filesystem.

Make sure all pkg_postinst script execution for installed packages is feasible during do_rootfs. This is required in case read-only-rootfs is in IMAGE_FEATURES.

It is important to highlight that one of the most common mistakes when creating post-installation scripts is the lack of the D variable in front of absolute paths. This ensures that paths are valid in both the host and target environments. Also, checking if the D variable is empty allows us to determine which environment is being used and possibly use different code if running during root filesystem generation or on a target.

Another common mistake is to attempt to run processes that are specific to or dependent on the target architecture. The easiest solution in this case is to postpone script execution of the target, but as mentioned before, this prevents the use of read-only filesystems.

Understanding shared state cache

The default behavior of Poky is to build everything from scratch unless BitBake determines that a recipe does not need to be rebuilt. The main advantage of building everything from scratch is that the final result is fresh and there is no risk of previous data causing problems. However, rebuilding everything requires computational time and resources.

The strategy to determine whether a recipe must be rebuilt is complex. Basically, BitBake tries to track as much information as possible about every task, variable, and code used in the build process. BitBake then generates a checksum for all the involved information for every task.

Poky uses all this information provided by BitBake to store snapshots of those tasks as a set of packaged data generated in a cache, which is called the shared state cache (`sstate-cache`). This cache wraps the contents of each task output in packages stored in the `SSTATE_DIR` directory. Whenever BitBake prepares to run a task, it first checks the existence of an `sstate-cache` package that matches. If the package is present, BitBake uses the prebuilt built package.

This is a very simple view of the whole shared state mechanism, which is quite a complex piece of code. For an advanced overview, it is advised that the Shared State Cache section of the Yocto Project Reference Manual is read. Please visit the following link for more information: `http://www.yoctoproject.org/docs/current/ref-manual/ref-manual.html`.

When using Poky for several builds, we must bear in mind that `sstate-cache` needs to be cleaned from time to time since it keeps growing as more and more cached data is added for every build. There is an easy way of cleaning it, as follows:

```
$ ./scripts/sstate-cache-management.sh --remove-duplicated -d --cache-
dir=<path to sstate-cached>
```

This removes the duplicated and old data from the cache.

> When we need to rebuild from scratch, we either remove the `build/tmp` so that we can use `sstate-cache` to speed up the build, or we remove both `build/tmp` and `sstate-cache` so that no cache is reused during the build.

Explaining package versioning

Package versioning is used to differentiate the same package in different stages of its life cycle. From Poky's perspective, it is also used as part of the equation that generates the checksum used by BitBake to verify whether a task must be rebuilt.

The package version, also known as PV, plays a central role when we select which recipe to build. The default behavior of Poky is to always prefer the newest recipe version, unless there is an explicit different preference, as we discussed in the Chapter 4, *Grasping the BitBake Tool*. For example, consider that we have two versions of the recipe myrecipe—myrecipe_1.0.bb and myrecipe_1.1.bb. BitBake, by default, builds the recipe with version 1.1.

Inside the recipe, we may have other variables that compose package versioning with the PV variable. These are package epoch, known as PE and package revision, known as PR.

The PE variable has a default value of zero and is used when the package version schema is changed, breaking the possibility of usual ordering. The package epoch is prepended in the package version, forcing a higher number when needed. For example, if a package uses the date to compose PV variables such as 20140101 and 20140201, the version schema is changed for a reason, and a new version, 1.0, is released, it is impossible to determine whether version 1.0 is higher than version 20140201. So, PE = "1" is used, forcing version 1.0 to be higher than 20140201 since 1:1.0 is greater than 0:20140101.

The PR variable has a default value of r0 and is used as part of package versioning. When it is updated, it forces BitBake to rebuild all tasks of a specific recipe. We can update it manually in the recipe metadata to force a rebuild we know is needed. Although the approach of manually setting the PR variables inside recipes may seem attractive, it is very fragile because it relies on human interaction and knowledge when it is required. Since *Yocto Project 1.5 (Dora)*, BitBake uses the task checksums to control what needs to be rebuilt, and the manual PR increment is only used in extremely rare cases when the task checksum does not change.

Specifying runtime package dependencies

The end results of most recipes are packages that are managed by the package manager. As we saw in the previous sections, it requires information about all those packages and how they relate to each other. For example, a package may depend on or conflict with another.

There are multiple package constraints that need to be expressed; however, those constraints are package format-specific, so BitBake has a specific metadata set used to abstract those package constraints.

Here is a list of the most commonly used runtime constraints:

- RDEPENDS: This is the list of packages that are required to be installed along with the package that defines it.
- RPROVIDES: This is the list of symbolic names a package provides. By default, a package always includes the package name as a symbolic name. It can also include other symbolic names alternatively provided by that package.
- RCONFLICTS: This is the list of packages that are known to conflict with this package. Only one of them can be installed at once.
- RREPLACES: This is a list of symbolic names that can be used as a replacement for this package.

Package feeds

As we discussed in Chapter 4, *Grasping the BitBake Tool*, packages play a central role, as images and SDKs rely on them. In fact, do_rootfs makes use of a local package repository to fetch the binary packages when generating the root filesystem. This repository is generally known as a *package feed*.

There is no reason for this repository to be used just for the images or SDK build steps. In fact, there are several valid reasons for making this repository remotely accessible internally in our development environment or publicly for use in the field. Some of these reasons are listed, including the following:

- Easily testing an updated application during development stage, without the need of a complete system re-installation
- Make additional packages more flexible so that they can be installed in a running image
- Update products in the field

To produce a solid package feed, we must ensure that we have consistent increments in the package revision every time the package is changed. It is almost impossible to do this manually, and the Yocto Project has a service, the *PR service*, specially designed to help in this area.

The PR service, which is part of BitBake, is used in order to increment the PR without human interaction every time BitBake detects a checksum change in a task. Essentially, it injects a suffix in PR in the format ${PR}.X. For example, considering PR = "r34" after subsequent PR service interactions, the PR value becomes r34.1, r34.2, r34.3, and so on.

When using Poky to generate images and not targeting a remote package feed, PR service is not required because BitBake triggers the required rebuilds due to the task checksum changes. The use of PR service is critical for solid package feeds, as it requires the version increase in a linear fashion.

 Even though we ought to use PR service to have a solid package versioning, it does not preclude the need to set PR manually in exceptional cases.

By default, the PR service is not enabled or running. To enable it to run locally, we must set the PRSERV_HOST variable in the BitBake configuration, for example, in build/conf/local.conf, as the following:

```
PRSERV_HOST = "localhost:0"
```

This approach is adequate when the build happens on a single computer, which builds every package of the package feed. BitBake starts and stops the server at each build and increases the required PR values automatically.

For a more complex setup, with multiple computers working against a common, shared package feed, we must have a single PR service running, which is used by all building systems associated with the package feed. In this case, we need to start the PR service in the server using the bitbake-prserv command, as shown here:

```
$ bitbake-prserv --host <ip> --port <port> --start
```

In addition to hand-starting the service, we need to update the BitBake configuration file (for example, build/conf/local.conf) of each build system, which connects to a server using the PRSERV_HOST variable as described earlier so that each system points to the server IP and port.

Using package feeds

In order to use package feeds, the following two components have to be configured properly:

- The server, to provide access to the packages
- The client, to access the server and download the required packages

The set of packages offered by the package feed is determined by the recipes we build. We can build one or more recipes and offer them, or we can build a set of images to generate the desired packages. Once we are satisfied with the set of packages offered, we must create the index of packages to be provided by the package feeds. This is performed by the following command:

```
$ bitbake package-index
```

The packages are available inside the build/tmp/deploy directory. We must choose the respective sub-directory depending on the package format chosen. Poky uses RPM by default so we must export the content of the build/tmp/deploy/rpm directory.

Make sure to run bitbake package-index after building all packages or those are not going to be included in the package database.

The package index, along with the packages, must be made available through a transfer protocol such as HTTP. We can use any server we wish for this task, such as Apache, Nginx, Lighttpd, and others. A convenient way to make the packages available through HTTP for local development is using the Python simple server, as shown here:

```
$ cd build/tmp/deploy/rpm
$ python3 -m http.server 5678
```

To add support for the package management onto the image, we have a couple of changes to do. We need to add package-management in EXTRA_IMAGE_FEATURES and set the URI for package fetching on PACKAGE_FEED_URIS. For example, we can add this to our build/conf/local.conf:

```
PACKAGE_FEED_URIS = "http://my-ip-address:5678"
EXTRA_IMAGE_FEATURES += " package-management "
```

We detail the IMAGE_FEATURES and EXTRA_IMAGE_FEATURES variables in Chapter 11, *Creating Custom Layers*. If we want a small image with no package management support, we should not include package-management in EXTRA_IMAGE_FEATURES.

The PACKAGE_FEED_URIS and EXTRA_IMAGE_FEATURES configurations guarantee that the image running on the client side can access the server and has the utilities needed in order to install, remove, and upgrade its packages.

After these steps have been taken, we are able to use the runtime package management in the target device.

For example, if we choose the RPM package format for the image, we can fetch the repository information using the following command:

```
$ dnf check-update
```

Use the dnf search <package> and dnf install <package> commands to find and install packages from the repositories.

Depending on the package format chosen, the commands for the target to update the package index, search, and install a package are different. See the available command lines for each package format in the following table:

Package format	RPM	IPK	DEB
Update the package index	dnf check-updates	opkg update	apt-get update
Search a package	dnf search <package>	opkg search <package>	apt-cache search <package>
Install a package	dnf install <package>	opkg install <package>	apt-get install <package>
System upgrade	dnf upgrade	opkg upgrade	apt-get dist-upgrade

The steps shown in this chapter are great for use in a local development phase because it enable us to install packages in an already deployed image.

The packages feed for system upgrade in the field requires a huge amount of work to test all different upgrade scenarios and to guarantee that the system does not fall into a broken state. Usually, full image upgrades are preferred for production use.

The management of a package feed is much more complex and involves several other aspects such as the package dependency chains, different upgrade scenarios, and more. The creation of a complex package feed external server is out of this book's scope so please refer to the Yocto Project documentation for further details.

Summary

This chapter presented the basic concept of packaging, a concept that has a central role for Poky and BitBake; package versioning; and how this impacts Poky's behavior when rebuilding packages and package feeds. It also showed us how to configure an image to be updated using prebuilt packages provided by a remote server.

In the next chapter, we will learn about the BitBake metadata syntax and its operators to `append`, `prepend`, and `remove` content from variables, variable expansions, and so on. We will then be able to understand the language used in Yocto Project engines better.

7
Diving into BitBake Metadata

At this point, we know how to generate images and packages, as well as how to use package feeds - basically everything we must know for simple usage of Poky. Hereafter, we will learn how to control the behavior of Poky to accomplish our goals and achieve maximum benefit from the Yocto Project as a whole.

In this chapter, we will enhance our understanding of the BitBake metadata syntax. We will learn to use the `append`, `prepend`, and `remove` operators to alter content from variables, variable expansions, and so on. These are the key concepts we can use to make our own recipes and customizations that we will learn about in `Chapter 10`, *Exploring External Layers*, `Chapter 11`, *Creating Custom Layers*, and `Chapter 12`, *Customizing Existing Recipes*.

Using metadata

The amount of metadata used by BitBake is enormous. To get the maximum benefit out of using Poky, we must master it. As we learned in `Chapter 4`, *Grasping the BitBake Tool*, metadata can be classified into the following three major areas:

- **Configuration** (the `.conf` files): Configuration files define the global content that is used to provide information and configure how the classes and recipes will work
- **Classes** (the `.bbclass` files): Classes are available to the whole system and can be inherited by recipes to easily maintain and avoid code duplication
- **Recipes** (the `.bb` or `.bbappend` files): The recipes describe the tasks to be run and provide the required information to allow BitBake to generate the required task chain. They are the most commonly used type of metadata as they are where we put it all at work. The most common types of recipes generate packages and images.

The classes and recipes are written in a mix of Python and shell scripting code. When a recipe is executed by BitBake, a local state is created so the inherited classes and recipe-specific metadata do not produce side effects elsewhere.

Working with metadata

The syntax used by BitBake metadata may be misleading, and can sometimes be hard to trace. We can check the value of each variable we want using the environment option (-e or --environment) of BitBake, for example:

```
$ bitbake -e <recipe> | grep <variable>
```

In order to understand how BitBake works in more detail, please refer to https://www.yoctoproject.org/docs/current/bitbake-user-manual/bitbake-user-manual.html.

In the following sections, we will see most of the syntax commonly used in recipes.

The basic variable setting

The assignment of a variable can be done as shown:

```
FOO = "bar"
```

In the preceding example, the value of the FOO variable is bar.

Variable assignment is core to the BitBake metadata syntax as most other examples are performed using variables.

Variable expansion

BitBake supports variable referencing. The syntax closely resembles Shell Script, for example:

```
A = "aval"
B = "pre${A}post"
```

This results in A containing aval and B containing preavalpost. One important thing to bear in mind is that the variable only expands when it is actually used, as shown:

```
A = "aval"
B = "pre${A}post"
A = "change"
```

The preceding example illustrates the *laziness* of BitBake evaluation. When B is used, it evaluates A (as it is a reference for it); A now contains a change, and B is prechangepost.

Setting a default value using ?=

When there is a need to provide a default value, the ?= operator can be used. The following code shows its use:

```
A ?= "aval"
```

If A is set before the preceding code is called, it retains its previous value; if A has not been previously set, it is set to aval. Basically, the ?= operator assigns a new value to a variable if one has not already been set.

Note that if there are multiple ?= assignments to a single variable, the first of these is used. For example, we may have the following:

```
A ?= "aval"
A ?= "change"
```

The variable A has the value aval. However, if we have A previously set, then it is used. For example:

```
A = "before"
A ?= "aval"
A ?= "change"
```

The A variable is kept as before.

Setting a default value using ??=

Another way to provide a default value is using the ??= operator. The difference between ??= and ?= is that with ??= the assignment does not occur until the end of the parsing process so that the last rather than the first ??= assignment to a given variable is used. Check the following code:

```
A ??= "somevalue"
A ??= "someothervalue"
```

If A is set before the preceding code, it retains the value. If A has not been previously set, it is set to someothervalue.

Immediate variable expansion

Use the `:=` operator when there is a need to force the immediate expansion of a variable. It results in the variable's contents being expanded immediately rather than when the variable is actually used, as follows:

```
T = "123"
A := "${B} ${A} test ${T}"
B = "${T} bval"
T = "456"
C = "cval"
C := "${C}append"
```

At the end of this example, `A` will contain `test 123`, `B` will contain `456 bval`, and `C` will be `cvalappend`. When `A` is expanded, `B` is not yet defined, so `B` is empty.

Appending and prepending

BitBake offers two sets of appending and prepending operators. The first are `+=` and `=+`. The following code illustrates their use:

```
B = "bval"
B += "additionaldata"
C = "cval"
C =+ "test"
```

At the end of this example, `B` contains `bval additionaldata` and `C` contains `test cval`. It is important to note that these operators include an extra space between each call.

When we wish to avoid adding spaces, we use the `.=` and `=.` operators. Look at the following code:

```
B = "bval"
B .= "additionaldata"
C = "cval"
C =. "test"
```

In this example, `B` is now `bvaladditionaldata` and `C` is `testcval`. In contrast to the preceding example, the `.=` and `=.` operators add no additional space. Commonly, the `+=` and `=+` operators are used to add items to lists while the `.=` and `=.` operators are used to concatenate strings.

Override syntax operators

You can also append and prepend a variable's value using an override-style syntax. For example:

```
B = "bval"
B_append "additionaldata"
C = "cval"
C_prepend "test"
```

In this example, B is now `bvaladditionaldata` and C is `testcval`. These operators add no additional space.

There is a subtle difference between how the appending and prepending operators are parsed. When using the extended operators, the expansion of the variables is forced prior to the operation to be executed so, for example:

```
A ?= "aval"
A .= "more"
B ?= "bval"
B_prepend = "more"
```

In the prior example, when the `.=` operator is run A is not expanded, and then A becomes `more`. In the case of B, before executing the `prepend` operation B is expanded so it becomes `morebval`.

Besides appending and prepending contents we can also intend to remove a variable's value, which can be done as follows:

```
A = "aval1 aval2 aval3"
A_remove = "aval1 aval3"
```

In this example, A value is now `aval2`. The `remove` operator considers the variable value as a list of strings separated by spaces, so the operator can remove one or more strings from this list.

Conditional metadata set

BitBake provides a very easy-to-use way to write conditional metadata. It is done by a mechanism called *overrides*.

The OVERRIDES variable contains values separated by colons (:), and each value is an item we want to satisfy conditions. So, if we have a variable that is conditional on arm, and arm is in OVERRIDES, then the version of the variable that is specific to arm is used rather than the non-conditional version, as shown:

```
OVERRIDES = "architecture:os:machine"
TEST = "defaultvalue"
TEST_os = "osspecificvalue"
TEST_other = "othercondvalue"
```

In this example, TEST will be osspecificvalue due to the condition of os being in OVERRIDES.

Conditional appending

BitBake also supports appending and prepending to variables based on whether something is in OVERRIDES, as shown here:

```
DEPENDS = "glibc ncurses"
OVERRIDES = "machine:local"
DEPENDS_append_machine = " libmad"
```

In the preceding example, DEPENDS is set to glibc ncurses libmad.

File inclusion

BitBake provides two directives for file inclusion: include and require.

With the first directive, include, BitBake attempts to insert the file at that location. If the path specified on the include line is a relative path, BitBake locates the first instance it can find within BBPATH. If the referenced file cannot be found, the parsing does not fail.

By contrast, the second directive, require, raises ParseError if the file to be included cannot be found. In all other aspects, it behaves just like the include directive.

> The convention normally adopted in the Yocto Project is to use a .inc file to share common code between two or more recipe files.

Python variable expansion

BitBake makes it easy to use Python code in variable expansion with the following syntax:

```
VARIABLE = "${@&lt;python-command>}"
```

This gives huge flexibility to the user, as can be seen in the following example:

```
DATE = "${@time.strftime('%Y%m%d',time.gmtime())}"
```

This results in the DATE variable containing today's date.

Defining executable metadata

Metadata recipes (.bb) and class files (.bbclass) can use Shell Script code as follows:

```
do_mytask () {
    echo "Hello, world!"
}
```

This is essentially identical to setting a variable, except that this variable happens to be an executable shell code. It is important to be careful when writing shell script code as we should not use shell-specific code such as bash or zsh. When in doubt, a good way to test if our code is safe is to use the dash shell to test it.

Another way to inject code is by using Python code, as shown:

```
python do_printdate () {
    import time
    print time.strftime('%Y%m%d', time.gmtime())
}
```

This is similar to the previous code but flags it as Python so that BitBake knows it is Python code and runs it accordingly.

Defining Python functions in the global namespace

We may be required to use Python functions to generate a value for a variable or some other use. This can be easily done, in recipes (.bb) and classes (.bbclass), using the following code:

```
def get_depends(d):
    if d.getVar('SOMECONDITION'):
        return "dependencywithcond"
    else:
        return "dependency"

SOMECONDITION = "1"
DEPENDS = "${@get_depends(d)}"
```

Usually, we need to access the BitBake database when writing a Python function. A convention among all metadata is that the d variable is used to point to BitBake's database, and it is usually passed as the last parameter of a function.

So, in the preceding example, we ask the database the value of the SOMECONDITION variable and return a value depending on it.

The example results in DEPENDS containing dependencywithcond.

The inheritance system

The inherit directive provides the means of specifying what classes of functionality our recipe (.bb) requires. It is a rudimentary form of inheritance. For example, we can easily abstract out the tasks involved in using autoconf and automake, and put them into .bbclass for our recipes to make use of. A given .bbclass is located by searching for classes/filename.bbclass in BBPATH, where filename is what we inherited. So, in a recipe that uses autoconf or automake, we can use the following:

```
inherit autotools
```

This instructs BitBake to inherit autotools.bbclass, so it provides the default tasks that work fine for most autoconf or automake based projects.

Summary

In this chapter, we learned in detail about the BitBake metadata syntax; its operators to `append`, `prepend`, and `remove` content from variables; variable expansions; and so on, including some usage examples for them.

In the next chapter, we will learn how to use Poky to create external compilation tools and produce a root filesystem suitable for in target development. In addition, the possible use of *Eclipse* integration will be explained.

8
Developing with the Yocto Project

So far, we have used Poky as a build tool; in other words, we have used it as a tool to design and generate the image that will be used on products. In this chapter, we will look at how the tool can help us with application or kernel development, create external compilation tools, produce a root filesystem suitable for cross development, and generate an image with the tools for use in the target machine for development.

Deciphering the software development kit

A **software development kit** (**SDK**) is a set of tools and files used to develop and debug. These tools include compilers, linkers, debuggers, external library headers, and binaries, and may include custom utilities and applications. This set of programming tools is called a toolchain.

In embedded development, the toolchain is often composed of cross-platform tools or tools executed on one architecture that then produces a binary for use in another architecture. For example, a gcc binary that runs on an x86-64-compatible machine and produces one binary for an ARM machine is a cross-compiler. When the tool and resultant binary are executed on the same architecture, it is called a native build.

Usually, when we work on custom source code and use external libraries, for example, libusb or libgl, these libraries are used to build at runtime. The custom source may be built against the library header files, and the binary may be moved somewhere during the execution. The set of files used at build time is placed under the sysroots directory, part of the Poky SDK, which is very configurable, depending on the application, and is a very simple one for general use.

When Poky executes tasks through the use of BitBake, it also needs a toolchain to be able to compile and link binaries for the target. This is called an internal toolchain because the tools are used internally by the build system. These tools are not intended to be used externally as they are not prepared for that, although they may be used in some very specific and advanced use cases.

Working with the Poky SDK

Usually, the standard Poky workflow includes creating package recipes and images, and deciding what will be installed on the final product image. However, a huge amount of time is spent developing, writing, testing, or adapting source code for our application.

When we write and test our application, we only care about the application itself, providing the libraries that the application requires before application development, although this can be an iterative process. However, we want a test environment that looks as similar as possible to the final one, mainly because of toolchain compatibility but also to avoid behavioral changes when we integrate the application into our product.

To help with this task, we can create a toolchain to be used externally with the Poky environment. Poky generates an SDK package that can be installed on any computer, regardless of whether Poky is installed on it. In addition, the installed toolchain is compatible with the internal one. Besides the toolchain, the SDK can also provide a set of library files (such as library binaries and header files), depending on our needs.

Using an image-based SDK

For custom source code, we know the dependency libraries and the other applications we depend on. In such cases, we can create an image that reflects our needs exactly or uses the closest image provided by Poky.

In order to create the image-based SDK, execute the following command:

```
$ bitbake core-image-full-cmdline -c populate_sdk
```

With this command, the SDK is created based on the `core-image-full-cmdline` image. If we have a custom image, we can use it instead. The SDK is generated to match the architecture of the machine we set using the `MACHINE` variable.

After the SDK is built, a binary script can be found at `build/tmp/deploy/sdk/poky-glibc-x86_64-core-image-full-cmdline-armv5e-toolchain-2.4.sh`.

Do not open the preceding script on a simple text editor. The script has a piece of binary code that may cause a text editor to crash

The resulting script should be installed before being used. We can see the installation process in the following screenshot:

```
●  -  □   Installation of sdk from build/tmp/deploy/sdk
Poky (Yocto Project Reference Distro) SDK installer version 2.4
================================================================
Enter target directory for SDK (default: /opt/poky/2.4):
You are about to install the SDK to "/opt/poky/2.4". Proceed[Y/n]? Y
Extracting SDK......................................done
Setting it up...done
SDK has been successfully set up and is ready to be used.
Each time you wish to use the SDK in a new shell session, you need to
source the environment setup script e.g.
 $ . /opt/poky/2.4/environment-setup-armv5e-poky-linux-gnueabi
$ █
```

In the preceding example, the installation directory was `/opt/poky/2.4`; however, we may choose any directory. The installation provides the following:

- `environment-setup-armv5te-poky-linux-gnueabi`: This is the script used to set up all environment variables needed to use the toolchain.
- `site-config-armv5te-poky-linux-gnueabi`: This is the file with the variables used during toolchain creation.
- `version-armv5te-poky-linux-gnueabi`: This is the version and timestamp information.
- `sysroots`: This is a copy of the `rootfs` directory of images used for SDK generation. It includes binary, header, and library files distributed across sub-directories such as:
    - `armv5te-poky-linux-gnueabi`: This contains files for ARM machines
    - `x86_64-pokysdk-linux`: These are files for machines with x86-64 compatibility

Generic SDK – meta-toolchain

Another option is to create a **generic SDK**, but with cross-compiler, debug tools, and a basic set of libraries and header files. This generic SDK is called **meta-toolchain**, and it is used mainly for kernel and bootloader development, and the debug process. In order to create it, use the following command:

```
$ bitbake meta-toolchain
```

The resultant file is `build/tmp/deploy/sdk/poky-eglibc-x86_64-meta-toolchain-armv5te-toolchain-2.4.sh` for the `qemuarm` machine. The installation process is exactly same as the image-based SDK.

Although this SDK is very helpful, it is highly recommended to create a custom image that fits our application needs, and then create the SDK based on this.

Using an SDK

To use an SDK to build a custom application, for example, `hello-world.c`, we can use the following lines, targeting the ARM architecture:

```
$ source /opt/poky/2.4/environment-setup-armv5e-poky-linux-gnueabi
$ ${CC} hello-world.c -o hello-world
```

In order to confirm that the generated binary was properly made for the target architecture, we can use the file utility as follows:

```
$ file hello-world
hello-world: ELF 32-bit LSB executable, ARM, EABI5 version 1 (SYSV),
dynamically linked, interpreter /lib/ld-linux.so.3, for GNU/Linux 3.2.0,
BuildID[sha1]=ce9b7de598f76a9611f98a4ce6b1af6018c0471b, not stripped
```

Another very commonly used project is the Linux kernel. The Linux kernel uses the LD utility for linking, so it is necessary to reset the LDFLAGS variable using the unset command so it returns to its default value, as defined for use with GCC. When we want to build the Linux kernel source code, we can use the following sequence of commands:

```
$ source /opt/poky/2.4/environment-setup-armv5e-poky-linux-gnueabi
$ unset LDFLAGS
$ make defconfig
$ make zImage
```

The Yocto Project **Extensible SDK (eSDK)** allows for distributed development as developers can update and extend the existing SDK environment during the project's lifetime. There is some infrastructure setup required for the proper use of eSDK as a sstate-cache mirror and eSDK server, which requires a complex configuration beyond the scope of this book. Please refer to `http://www.yoctoproject.org/docs/2.4/sdk-manual/sdk-manual.html`

Developing applications on the target

For embedded systems, there is a debug portion that should be executed on real hardware because the application uses hardware-specific peripherals, and it may be difficult to emulate them. In addition, some of the debug processes are dependent on source signals, electrical or optical, otherwise the resultant action will be a mechanical behavior that may be difficult to test effectively on emulators.

The first proposed scenario for the development on the target system is to create a development image to be used along with an external toolchain. A development image is filled with header files and additional library links. This will be an image that is prepared to provide a build environment for a custom application, and it may be used with a custom toolchain or the Yocto Project external toolchain. The following line adds these properties to an image:

```
IMAGE_FEATURES += "dev-pkgs"
```

In case we want to modify only `build/conf/local.conf`, the variable to be used is `EXTRA_IMAGE_FEATURES`. The `IMAGE_FEATURES` variable is better described in `Chapter 11`, *Creating Custom Layers*.

The resulting image includes header files and additional library links, and it may be used during the custom application development cycle. The custom application may be built against this images root filesystem, which means that the image itself does not need to be recreated each time. In addition, the image may be shared among all developers working on the same project. Each one will have a copy, and everyone will be on the same page.

The `dev-pkgs` features install all `${PN}-dev` packages into the image.

For developers who prefer, or need, to use a native build instead of creating a development build, Poky can be configured to generate an SDK image. This image contains the toolchain and development packages (header files and library links). It means we can have the source code of our custom application being built, run, tested, and debugged on the target machine.

In order to add the development tools inside an image, we need to include the `tools-sdk` feature in the `IMAGE_FEATURES` variable. We should use `EXTRA_IMAGE_FEATURES` if it is added in `build/conf/local.conf`.

 Bear in mind that lately there are new processors that have been developed for specific markets that may provide completely different resource sets (processing, peripherals, memory, and so on).

A native build is a good option when we have a microprocessor that provides reasonable performance, and our device has enough memory for the native build to be feasible. The resources needed for a native build vary greatly from one library or application to another.

Integrating with Eclipse

Eclipse is a very powerful IDE, and is widely used for the development and debugging of custom applications. It can be configured to work with the Poky SDK. In the Yocto Project SDK Developer's Guide at `http://www.yoctoproject.org/docs/2.4/sdk-manual/sdk-manual.html`, we can find the supported Eclipse version and can learn how to configure it. Included in the manual are the Yocto Project ADT and an image based on generic toolchain integration.

As soon as our Eclipse is configured, we can use it for development. We can use the IDE to write the source code, and the Poky toolchain can be used to cross-compile it, as Eclipse supports the use of this external toolchain.

In addition, we can use Eclipse to deploy the generated binary file to the target, connected with Eclipse by Ethernet. The binary file and any other required artifacts are copied to the target root filesystem, and it is possible to use the filesystem right after the transfer.

As soon as the binary is copied to the root filesystem, we can use Eclipse to debug the application. This means that we are allowed to use step-by-step debugging, with the binary being run directly on the target machine.

In order to accomplish Eclipse integration, it's important to include the Eclipse feature in the target image by adding the following piece of code in `build/conf/local.conf`:

```
IMAGE_FEATURES += "eclipse-debug"
```

 The authors of this book decided not to include a step-by-step guide to how to get Eclipse installed and configured because it requires several steps and will become outdated very fast. The website `http://www.yoctoproject.org/docs/2.4/sdk-manual/sdk-manual.html`, on the other hand, contains a complete and up-to-date tutorial for that.

Summary

In this chapter, we learned that the Yocto Project can be used for development as well as for image creation. We learned how to create two types of toolchains, image-based and generic, how to use them, and how to create a development image in order to build and deploy our application on the target machine. In addition, we learned how we can use Eclipse in the development phase to write, build, and debug our applications.

In the next chapter, we will look at how we can configure Poky to help us in the debugging process, how we can configure our system to provide the required tools for a remote debug using GDB, how we can track our changes using `buildhistory`, and how we can use a handy tool called `devshell`.

9
Debugging with the Yocto Project

The debug process is an important step in every development cycle. In this chapter, we will understand how to configure Poky to help us with the debugging process, for example, how we can configure our system to provide the tools needed for a remote debug using GDB, how we can track our changes using `buildhistory`, and how we can use a handy tool called devshell.

Differentiating metadata and application debugging

When we first think about debugging, we usually don't realize that there are different types of debugging.

Metadata debugging is needed to ensure that the behavior of BitBake's tasks is aligned with our goals, and to identify the culprit when it's not. In this case, we use several log files generated by BitBake in the host in order to help trace the execution path of the involved task. As a consequence of a wrong behavior, a file may not be copied or a feature may not be enabled.

On the other hand, the debugging of runtime code is more natural for us as it is essentially the same as what we do during the normal development cycle of an application, a library, or a kernel. Depending on the kind of issue we are after, the right tool to help may vary from a debugger to code instrumentation (for example, adding debug prints).

In this chapter, we detail metadata debugging as it is the essence of the Yocto Project and supports us during the development and use of Poky.

Tracking image, package, and SDK contents

The easiest way to ensure we have the image, packages, and SDK, along with the expected contents, is to use the **Build History** mechanism.

When a recipe is updated for a new version or has its code changed, it may influence the contents put in the generated packages and, as a consequence, in the image or SDK.

As Poky deals with a huge amount of recipes, and our images or SDKs frequently have tens or hundreds of packages included, it may be quite difficult to track the package contents. The Poky tool responsible for helping us in this task is the Build History.

The Build History, as we can guess from its name, keeps a history of the contents of several artifacts built during the use of Poky. It can track package, image, and SDK building.

To enable the Build History in our system, we need to add the following lines of code in our `build/conf/local.conf` file:

```
INHERIT += "buildhistory"
BUILDHISTORY_COMMIT = "1"
```

The `INHERIT` method includes the `buildhistory` class hooks in the building process, while the `BUILDHISTORY_COMMIT` line enables BitBake to create a new Git commit in the `buildhistory` repository for every new package, image, or SDK build. This makes the track as simple as `git diff` between two commits.

The data for all packages, images, and SDKs built is stored under the `build/buildhistory` directory as text files so that it is easy to use this data to extract extra information. Poky provides a utility that outputs the difference between two `buildhistory` states, called `buildhistory-diff`, in a more concise way, which is very useful when checking for changes.

The `buildhistory-diff` utility outputs the difference between any two Git revisions in a more meaningful way. We can see an example of its output in the following screenshot:

```
 * – □  buildhistory-diff output
$ ../scripts/buildhistory-diff
Changes to images/qemuarm/glibc/core-image-minimal (files-in-image.txt):
  /usr/bin/strace-log-merge was added
  /usr/bin/strace was added
  * (installed-package-names.txt):
  *    strace was added
  *    * IMAGE_INSTALL: added "strace"
images/qemuarm/glibc/core-image-minimal: IMAGE_INSTALL: added "strace"
images/qemuarm/glibc/core-image-minimal: IMAGESIZE changed from 6728 to 7172 (+6%)
Changes to images/qemuarm/glibc/core-image-minimal (installed-package-names.txt):
  strace was added
  * IMAGE_INSTALL: added "strace"
$ 
```

The preceding screenshot shows the differences highlighted by `buildhistory-diff` when the `strace` package is added in the `core-image-minimal` image.

When a package is built, `buildhistory` creates a list of generated sub-packages, installation scripts, a list of file ownership and sizes, the dependency relation, and more. For images and SDKs, the dependency relationship among the packages, filesystem files, and dependency graph is created.

For a better understanding of all capabilities and features provided by `buildhistory`, you are advised to read the following source: `http://www.yoctoproject.org/docs/2.4/ref-manual/ref-manual.html`

Debugging packaging

In more sophisticated recipes, we split the installed contents into several sub-packages. The sub-packages can be optional features, modules, or any other set of files that it is optional to install.

To inspect how the recipe's content has been split, we can use the `build/tmp/work/<arch>/<recipe name>/<software version>/packages-split` directory. It contains a sub-directory for every sub-package and has its contents in the sub-tree.

Among the possible reasons for a mistaken content split, we have the following:

- Contents not being installed (for example, an error in installation scripts)
- Application or library configuration error (for example, a disabled feature)
- Metadata error (for example, wrong package order)

Another common issue that we find, mainly in library recipes, is that the required artifacts are not made available in the `sysroot` directory (for example, headers or dynamic libraries), causing a build breakage. The counterpart of the `sysroot` generation can be seen at `build/tmp/work/<arch>/<recipe name>/<software version>/sysroot-destdir`.

Other possible causes may need us to instrument the task code with the further presented logging functions, so we can figure out the logical error or bug that causes the unexpected result.

Logging information during task execution

The logging utilities provided by BitBake are very useful for tracing the code execution path. BitBake provides logging functions for use in Python and Shell Script code, described as follows:

- **Python**: For use within Python functions, BitBake supports several log levels, which are `bb.fatal`, `bb.error`, `bb.warn`, `bb.note`, `bb.plain`, and `bb.debug`
- **Shell Script**: For use in Shell Script functions, the same set of log levels exists and is accessed with a similar syntax: `bbfatal`, `bberror`, `bbwarn`, `bbnote`, `bbplain`, and `bbdebug`

These logging functions are very similar to each other but have inner differences, described as follows:

- `bb.fatal` and `bbfatal`: These have the highest priority of logging messages as they print the message and terminate the processing. They cause the build to be interrupted.
- `bb.error` and `bberror`: These are used to display an error but do not force the build to stop.
- `bb.warn` and `bbwarn`: These are used to warn users about something.

- `bb.note` and `bbnote`: These add a note to the user. They are only informative.
- `bb.plain` and `bbplain`: These output a message.
- `bb.debug` and `bbdebug`: These add debugging information that is shown depending on the debug level used.

There is one subtle difference between the use of the logging functions in Python and Shell Scripting.

The logging functions in Python are directly handled by BitBake, seen on the console, and stored in the execution log that can be seen inside `build/tmp/log/cooker/<machine>`.

When the logging functions are used in Shell Script, the information is outputted to the task's respective task log file, which is available in `build/tmp/work/<arch>/<recipe name>/<software version>/temp`.

Inside it, we can run the scripts for every task with the `run.<task>.<pid>` pattern and use the `log.<task>.<pid>` pattern for its output. For convenience, symbolic links are kept updated by BitBake, pointing to the last log files using the `log.<task>` pattern; thus, we can actually check for `log.do_compile`, for example, when intending to verify whether the right files were used during the build process. Alternatively, we can check for `log.do_patch` to verify whether a patch has been applied.

The `build/tmp/work` directory is detailed in Chapter 5, *Detailing the Temporary Build Directory*.

Utilizing a development shell

When editing packages or debugging build failures, a development shell can be a useful tool. When we use `devshell`, source files are extracted into the working directory, patches are applied, a new terminal is opened, and files are placed in the working directory.

In the new terminal, all the environment variables needed for the build are still defined, so we can use commands such as `configure` and `make`. The commands execute just as if the build system was executing them.

The following command is an example that uses `devshell` on a target named `linux-yocto`:

```
$ bitbake linux-yocto -c devshell
```

This allows us to rework the Linux kernel source code and build it in place, to avoid building it from scratch on our development machine, and change its code as needed.

 It is important to bear in mind that no changes made inside `devshell` are persistent between builds; thus, we must be careful to record any change that is important, prior to leaving it.

As we have the source at our disposal, we can use it to generate extra patches. One very practical way of doing that is using Git and `git format-patch` to create the patch to be included in the recipe afterward. The following screenshot shows the devshell window open after calling the `devshell` task:

```
⚉  –  ◻  devshell example
$ bitbake linux-yocto -c devshell
Loading cache: 100% |############################################################################| Time: 0:00:06
Loaded 1275 entries from dependency cache.
NOTE: Resolving any missing task queue dependencies

Build Configuration:
BB_VERSION        = "1.35.0"
BUILD_SYS         = "x86_64-linux"
NATIVELSBSTRING   = "universal"
TARGET_SYS        = "arm-poky-linux-gnueabi"
MACHINE           = "qemuarm"
DISTRO            = "poky"
DISTRO_VERSION    = "2.4"
TUNE_FEATURES     = "arm armv5 thumb dsp"
TARGET_FPU        = "soft"
meta
meta-poky
meta-yocto-bsp    = "rocko:65d23bd7986615fdfb0f1717b615534a2a14ab80"

Initialising tasks: 100% |###############  ⚉  –  ◻   Terminal
NOTE: Executing SetScene Tasks          $ ls
NOTE: Executing RunQueue Tasks          arch      CREDITS        firmware  ipc       lib          net       security  virt
Currently  1 running tasks (286 of 286) block     crypto         fs        Kbuild    MAINTAINERS  README    sound
0: linux-yocto-4.12.12+gitAUTOINC+eda4d18 certs    Documentation  include   Kconfig   Makefile     samples   tools
□                                        COPYING   drivers        init      kernel    mm           scripts   usr
                                         $ export | grep ARCH
                                         declare -x ARCH="arm"
                                         declare -x UBOOT_ARCH="arm"
                                         $ ▮
```

The `devshell` is convenient for small tasks but when a more involved change is needed, use an external toolchain in a normal development cycle and then integrate the resulting patches in the recipe.

In order to include the generated patch in the recipe and make it persistent, see Chapter 12, *Customizing Existing Recipes*.

Using the GNU Project Debugger for debugging

While developing any project, from time to time we end up struggling to understand subtle bugs. The **GNU Project Debugger** (**GDB**) is available as a package within Poky and is installed in SDK images by default, as was detailed in Chapter 8, *Developing with the Yocto Project*.

 In order to install debugging packages that contain the debug symbols and debugging tools in an image, add IMAGE_FEATURES += "dbg-pkgs tools-debug" in build/conf/local.conf.

The use of the SDK, or an image with the debugging packages and tools installed, allows us to debug applications directly in the target, as we usually do on our development machine.

The GDB may not be usable on some targets because of memory or disk space constraints. The main reason for this limitation is the GDB needs to load the debugging information, along with the binaries of the process being debugged, before starting the debugging process.

To overcome these constraints, we can use gdbserver, included by default when using tools-debug in IMAGE_FEATURES. It runs on the target and doesn't load any debugging information from the debugged process. Instead, a GDB instance processes the debugging information on the host. The host GDB then sends control commands to gdbserver to control the debugged application.

As the host GDB is responsible for loading the debugging information and performing the necessary processing to make the debugging process take place, the target does not need to have the debugging symbols installed and we need to make sure the host can access the binaries with their debugging information. It is advisable that the target binaries are compiled with no optimizations to facilitate the debugging process.

The process to use gdbserver and configure the host and target in the appropriate way is detailed on the following site: http://www.yoctoproject.org/docs/2.4/dev-manual/dev-manual.html.

Summary

In this chapter, we understood how we can configure Poky to help us with the debugging process. We learned the contents of deployed directories that can be used for debugging, how we can track our changes using buildhistory, how we can use devshell to emulate the same build environment found by BitBake, and how we configure our system to provide the tools needed for GDB debugging.

In the next chapter, we will understand how to expand the Poky source code using external layers. We will be introduced to the concept of layering, and we will learn in detail the directory structure and the content of each layer type.

10
Exploring External Layers

One of the most charming features of Poky is the flexibility of using external layers. In this chapter, we will look at why this is a strong capability and how we can take advantage of this. We will look at the different layer types and how their directory trees are organized. Finally, we will learn how to include a new layer in our project.

Powering flexibility with layers

Poky contains a great amount of metadata spread over machine definition files, classes, and recipes. This metadata covers everything from simple applications to full graphical stacks and frameworks. BitBake has the ability to load metadata from multiple places, and those multiple metadata sets are known as metadata layers.

The biggest strength of using layers is the ability to split the metadata into logical units, which enables users to pick only the metadata set needed for the project. Using metadata layers improves the reuse of code and the ability to share work across different teams, communities, and vendors, increasing the code quality of the Yocto Project community as multiple entities are working together on the same metadata.

We may want to configure the system for different reasons, such as the need to enable/disable a feature or change build flags to enable architecture-specific optimizations. These are examples of customizations that can be done using layers.

In addition, when creating our own custom project environment, instead of changing recipes and configuration files, and modifying files in the Poky layer, we ought to organize the metadata in different layers. The more separated the organization is, the easier it is to reuse the layers in future projects; because of this fact, the Poky source code itself is also separated into different layers. It has three layers included by default, as we can see in the output of the following command line:

```
$ bitbake-layers show-layers
```

The result can be seen in the following screenshot:

```
*  -  □  Included layers
$ bitbake-layers show-layers
NOTE: Starting bitbake server...
layer                    path                                                    priority
========================================================================
meta                     /media/disco2/root_for_user_boot_ed2/poky/meta   5
meta-poky                /media/disco2/root_for_user_boot_ed2/poky/meta-poky   5
meta-yocto-bsp           /media/disco2/root_for_user_boot_ed2/poky/meta-yocto-bsp   5
$ ▮
```

The command-line output shows the following three important properties of any layer:

- **Name**: This usually starts with the `meta` string.
- **Path**: This is important when we want to add an additional layer in our project that is appended to the `BBPATH` variable.
- **Priority**: This is the value used by BitBake to decide which recipe to use and the order in which the `.bbappend` files should be joined. It means that if two layers include the same recipe file (`.bb`), the one with the highest priority is used. In the case of `.bbappen`, every `.bbappend` file is included in the original recipe, and the layer priority determines the order of inclusion, so the `.bbappend` files within the highest priority layers are appended first, followed by the others.

Poky is arranged in three individual layers, coincidentally the three types available. The `meta` layer is the OpenEmbedded Core metadata, which contains the recipes, classes, and the QEMU machine configuration files. It is a software layer.

A software layer includes only applications or configuration files for applications and can be used on any architecture. There is a huge list of software layers. To name only a few, we have `meta-java`, `meta-qt5`, and `meta-browser`. The `meta-java` layer provides Java runtime and SDK support, the `meta-qt5` layer includes Qt5 support, and `meta-browser` supports several web browsers such as Firefox and Chrome.

The `meta-yocto-bsp` layer is the Poky reference **board support package** (**BSP**) layer. It contains machine configuration files and recipes to configure packages for the machines. As it is a reference BSP layer, it can be used as an example.

The `meta-poky` layer is the Poky reference distribution layer. It contains a distribution configuration used in Poky by default; this is an example of a distribution file. This default distribution is described in the `poky.conf` file, and it is widely used for testing products. However, sometimes your product may have special needs, and changes in `build/conf/local.conf` will need to be made as required.

The `build/conf/local.conf` file is a volatile file that is not supposed to be tracked by Git.

We should not rely on it to set package versions, providers, and the system features for products, but use it just as a shortcut for testing purposes during development.

The most adequate and maintainable solution is to create a distribution layer to place the distribution definition file. This configuration allows any build to be reproduced afterward. We can use one distribution layer for all the distributions we have, or we can create one new layer for every new distribution; the best approach depends on your project's needs.

The policy configuration provided in a distribution layer overrides the same configuration from `build/conf/local.conf`.

Detailing the layer's source code

Usually, a layer has a directory tree, as shown in the following screenshot:

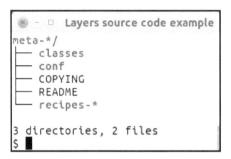

The layer name should start with `meta-`; it is not a requirement, but the advised naming convention. Inside this directory, there are two files, `<layer>/COPYING` and `<layer>/README`, a license, and a message to the user. In `<layer>/README`, we must specify any other dependency and information that the layer's users need to know.

The `classes` folder should hold both the classes provided the classes that are specific to that layer (the `.bbclass` files). It is an optional directory.

The `<layer>/conf` folder is mandatory and should provide the configuration files (the `.conf` files). Primarily, the layer configuration file `<layer>/conf/layer.conf`, to be detailed in the next chapter, is the file with the layer definition.

When the `<layer>/conf` folder is from a BSP layer, the directory structure should look like the following screenshot:

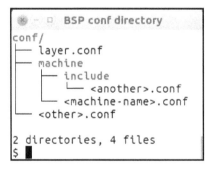

If the `<layer>/conf` folder is from a distribution layer, the directory structure should look like the following screenshot:

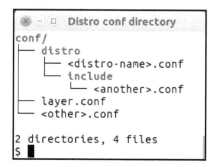

The `recipe-*` folder is a cluster of recipes separated by category, for example, `recipes-core`, `recipes-bsp`, `recipes-graphic`, `recipes-multimedia`, and `recipes-kernel`. Inside each folder, starting with `recipes-`, there is a directory with the recipe name or a group of recipes; inside it, the recipe files end with `.bb` or `.bbappend`. For example, we can find the following screenshot from `meta`:

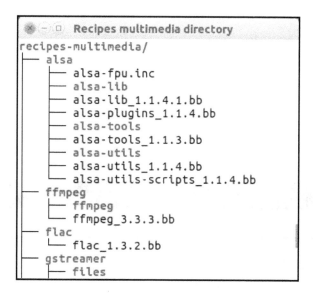

Adding meta layers

There are hundreds of meta layers from the Yocto Project, OpenEmbedded, communities, and companies that should be manually cloned inside the project source directory to be used. We can find them at `http://git.yoctoproject.org/` or `http://layers.openembedded.org`.

In order to include, for example, `meta-openembedded` in our project, we can change the content of the configuration files or use BitBake command lines. To do so, we need first to fetch the layer's source code. Please run the following command from your Poky source directory:

```
$ git clone git://git.openembedded.org/meta-openembedded -b rocko
```

We can now add a new layer by changing the `build/conf/bblayer.conf` file and adding the absolute path to the new meta layer directory, as shown in the following source code. The highlighted line is the one to be added. The others are the default values for this file:

```
build/conf/bblayers.conf content
# POKY_BBLAYERS_CONF_VERSION is increased each time build/conf/bblayers.conf
# changes incompatibly
POKY_BBLAYERS_CONF_VERSION = "2"

BBPATH = "${TOPDIR}"
BBFILES ?= ""

BBLAYERS ?= " \
  /home/user/poky/meta \
  /home/user/poky/meta-poky \
  /home/user/poky/meta-yocto-bsp \
  "

BBLAYERS += \
  /home/user/poky/meta-openembedded/meta-oe \
"
$
```

An alternative to manually editing `build/conf/bblayers.conf` is to use the `bitbake-layers` tool to do the inclusion for us. This can be done using the following command from the build directory:

```
$ bitbake-layers add-layer ../meta-openembedded/meta-oe
```

In the previous BitBake command, the added layer is parsed and the `meta-openembedded/meta-oe` metadata is included in BitBake's database, allowing the packages inside the added layer to be used.

The Yocto Project layer ecosystem

Because of the convenience of making a layer, there are a huge number of layers to use. To make all those available layers easier to access, the OpenEmbedded community has developed an index where most of them can be found.

Let's say we just ordered a Raspberry Pi 3 board; we can use the link to `https://layers.openembedded.org` and search for it in the **Machines** tab, as shown in the following screenshot:

Another very handy use case for the tools is to search for a specific software type or a recipe. It can save the day! We can see some commonly used layers in the following screenshot:

Summary

In this chapter, we introduced the concept of layering. We learned about the directory structure in detail and the content of each layer type. In addition, we saw how to add an external layer to our project manually or by using the BitBake command line, as well as how to make use of the OpenEmbedded Layer index to easily find the available layers that we need.

In the next chapter, we will learn more about why we need to create new layers and what the common metadata included in them is (such as machine definition files, recipes, and images), and wrap it all up with an example of distribution customization.

11
Creating Custom Layers

Beyond using existing layers from the community or from vendors, we learn why we create layers for our own products in this chapter. In addition, we discover how to create a machine definition and a distribution, and profit from them to better organize our source code.

Making a new layer

Before creating our own layer, it's always a good idea to check whether there is a similar one already available at the following website: `http://layers.openembedded.org`. If we cannot find a suitable layer for our needs, the next step is to create the directory. Usually, the layer name starts with `meta-`, but this is not a technical restriction.

The layer configuration file is required in every layer, and is placed in `<layer>/conf/layer.conf`; we can create it manually using any text editor, or populate it with a script provided in Poky, as shown in the following command:

```
$ ./poky/scripts/yocto-layer create newlayer
```

The output is shown in the following screenshot:

```
* - □  Creating a new layer meta-newlayer
$ ./poky/scripts/yocto-layer create newlayer
Please enter the layer priority you'd like to use for the layer: [default: 6]
Would you like to have an example recipe created? (y/n) [default: n] y
Please enter the name you'd like to use for your example recipe: [default: example]
Would you like to have an example bbappend file created? (y/n) [default: n] y
Please enter the name you'd like to use for your bbappend file: [default: example]
Please enter the version number you'd like to use for your bbappend file (this should
match the recipe you're appending to): [default: 0.1]

New layer created in meta-newlayer.

Don't forget to add it to your BBLAYERS (for details see meta-newlayer/README).
$ █
```

With the script, we are asked to enter the value for layer priority and answer other questions regarding the sample content that can be generated for the layer. We can use the default values, or enter a custom one. An example of a generated layer is shown in the following figure:

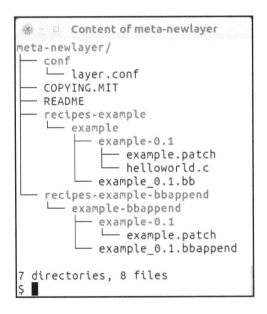

```
* - □  Content of meta-newlayer
meta-newlayer/
├── conf
│   └── layer.conf
├── COPYING.MIT
├── README
├── recipes-example
│   └── example
│       ├── example-0.1
│       │   ├── example.patch
│       │   └── helloworld.c
│       └── example_0.1.bb
└── recipes-example-bbappend
    └── example-bbappend
        ├── example-0.1
        │   └── example.patch
        └── example_0.1.bbappend

7 directories, 8 files
$ █
```

Important variables that may need to be added in case our layer requires other layers to work are as follows:

- LAYERVERSION: This is an optional variable that specifies the version of the layer in a single number. This variable is used within the LAYERDEPENDS variable in order to depend on a specific version of a layer, and it must be suffixed with the layer's name, for example, LAYERVERSION_newlayer = "1".
- LAYERDEPENDS: This lists the layers that the recipes depend upon, separated by spaces. Optionally, we can assign a specific layer version for a dependency by adding it to the end of the layer name with a colon, for example, otherlayer:2. This variable must be suffixed with the name of the specific layer, for example, LAYERDEPENDS_newlayer = "otherlayer".

If a dependency cannot be satisfied, or the version numbers do not match, an error is raised. The base of the layer structure is now created. In the following sections, we will learn how to extend it.

Adding metadata to the layer

The purpose behind the use of layers is to add extra metadata to BitBake's database, or change it.

The most commonly added features are project related, such as applications, libraries, or a service server.

On the other hand, instead of adding new features, it is much more common to accommodate existing feature configurations to our needs, for example, the initial network values for a SSH server, or the custom boot splash image.

It means that we can include several types of metadata files on a new layer— recipes, images, and bbappend files—to change existing features. The script used to create the new layer can also create two example files: the first one, example_0.1.bb, is a recipe example; the second one, example_0.1.bbappend, is a bbappend example used to modify the feature included in example_0.1.bb. There are several other examples of bbappend files on meta-yocto-bsp and meta-yocto, and we explore some of their common uses in the next chapter.

Creating an image

Image files can be seen as a set of packages grouped for a purpose and configured in a controlled way. We can either create a new image, including an existing image, adding the needed packages, or overriding configurations, or we can create the image from scratch.

When an image mostly fits our needs and we need to make only minor adjustments to it, it is very convenient to reuse its code. This makes code maintenance easier, and highlights the functional differences. For example, if we want to include an application and remove an image feature from `core-image-sato`, we can create an image at `recipes-mine/images/my-image-sato.bb` with the following lines of code:

```
require recipes-sato/image/core-image-sato.bb
IMAGE_FEATURES_remove = "splash"
CORE_IMAGE_EXTRA_INSTALL += "myapp"
```

On the other hand, we sometimes want to create our image from scratch; we can facilitate our work using the `core-image` class, as it provides a set of image features that can be used very easily, for example, an image in `recipes-mine/images/myimage-nano.bb` consists of the following lines of code:

```
inherit core-image
IMAGE_FEATURES += "ssh-server-openssh splash"
CORE_IMAGE_EXTRA_INSTALL += "nano"
```

The append operator (+=) is used to guarantee that a new `IMAGE_FEATURES` variable can be added by `build/conf/local.conf`.

`CORE_IMAGE_EXTRA_INSTALL` is the variable we should use to include extra packages into the image when we inherit the `core-image` class that facilitates image creation. This adds support for the `IMAGE_FEATURES` variable, which avoids a lot of duplication of code. The `IMAGE_INSTALL` variable groups the `CORE_IMAGE_EXTRA_INSTALL` contents, and `IMAGE_FEATURES`-related packages generate our root filesystem.

Currently, the following are the image features supported :

- `allow-empty-password`: Allows Dropbear and OpenSSH to accept root logins and logins from accounts with an empty password string
- `dbg-pkgs`: Installs debug symbol packages for all packages installed in a given image

- `debug-tweaks`: Makes an image suitable for development
- `dev-pkgs`: Installs development packages (headers and extra library links) for all packages installed in a given image
- `doc-pkgs`: Installs documentation packages for all packages installed in a given image
- `eclipse-debug`: Provides Eclipse IDE remote debugging support
- `empty-root-password`: Sets the root password to an empty string, which allows logins with a blank password
- `hwcodecs`: Installs hardware acceleration codecs
- `nfs-server`: Installs an NFS server
- `package-management`: Installs package management tools and preserves the package manager database
- `perf`: Installs profiling tools such as `perf`, `systemtap`, and `LTTng`
- `post-install-logging`: Enables logging post-install script runs to the `/var/log/postinstall.log` file on first boot of the image on the target system
- `ptest-pkgs`: Installs `ptest` packages for all ptest-enabled recipes
- `read-only-rootfs`: Creates an image whose root filesystem is read-only
- `splash`: Enables showing a splash screen during boot
- `ssh-server-dropbear`: Installs the Dropbear minimal SSH server
- `ssh-server-openssh`: Installs the OpenSSH server, which is more full-featured than Dropbear
- `staticdev-pkgs`: Installs static development packages, which are static libraries (that is, `*.a` files) for all packages installed in a given image
- `tools-debug`: Installs debugging tools such as `strace` and `gdb`
- `tools-sdk`: Installs a full SDK that runs on the device
- `tools-testapps`: Installs device testing tools (for example, touchscreen debugging)
- `x11`: Installs the X server
- `x11-base`: Installs the X server with a minimal environment
- `x11-sato`: Installs the OpenedHand Sato environment

Adding a package recipe

A package recipe is how we can instruct BitBake to fetch, unpack, compile, and install our application, kernel module, or any software provided by a project. Poky includes several classes that abstract the process for the most common development tools as projects based on Autotools, CMake, and QMake. A list of classes included in Poky can be seen in the following reference manual: http://www.yoctoproject.org/docs/2.4/ref-manual/ref-manual.html.

One simple recipe that executes the compile and install tasks explicitly is provided as follows:

```
DESCRIPTION = "Simple helloworld application"
SECTION = "examples"
LICENSE = "MIT"
LIC_FILES_CHKSUM = "file://${COMMON_LICENSE_DIR}/MIT;md5=0835ade698e0b
cf8506ecda2f7b4f302"
SRC_URI = "file://helloworld.c"
S = "${WORKDIR}"
do_compile() {
    ${CC} helloworld.c -o helloworld
}
do_install() {
    install -d ${D}${bindir}
    install -m 0755 helloworld ${D}${bindir}
}
```

The do_compile and do_install code blocks provide the Shell Scripting commands to build and install the resulting binary into the destination directory that is referenced as ${D}.

However, in the case of an Autotools-based project, we can avoid a lot of code duplication using the autotools class in the stripped example extracted from the recipe poky/meta/recipes-core/dbus-wait/dbus-wait_git.bb, as follows:

```
DESCRIPTION = "A simple tool to wait for a specific signal over DBus"
...
inherit autotools
```

The simple act of inheriting the class is, in fact, providing all the code required to do the following tasks:

- Update the configure script code and artefacts
- Update the libtool scripts
- Run the configure script
- Run Make
- Run Make install

The same concepts apply to other building tools, as is the case for CMake and QMake. The number of supported classes is growing, and it is expected that new ones will be included in every release to support new build systems and avoid code duplication.

Automatically creating a base package recipe using recipetool

The `recipetool` allows for easier creation of a base recipe based on the source code files. As long as you can extract or point to the source files, the `recipetool` will generate a recipe and automatically configure all pre-built information into the new recipe file.

To illustrate, assume we have an application that builds using Autotools. When we use the `recipetool` to create the base recipe, it generates a recipe that has the pre-build dependencies, it inherits the `autotools` class, sets the license requirements, and checksums.

The `recipetool` creates a recipe file with several comments that are intended for our understanding of the content. All the comments can be deleted when we integrate the recipe file to our metalayer.

To generate a recipe using the `bbexample`, available in `https://github.com/OSSystems/bbexample`, we can use the following commands:

```
$ source oe-init-build-env build
$ recipetool create -V 1.0 https://github.com/OSSystems/bbexample
```

The following image shows the recipe creation:

```
⚙ − □   Using recipetool to ease the recipe creation
$ recipetool create -V 1.0 https://github.com/OsSystems/bbexample
NOTE: Starting bitbake server...
NOTE: Fetching git://github.com/OsSystems/bbexample;protocol=https...
Loading cache: 100% |###############################################################| Time: 0:00:00
Loaded 1275 entries from dependency cache.
Parsing recipes: 100% |#############################################################| Time: 0:00:00
Parsing of 819 .bb files complete (818 cached, 1 parsed). 1276 targets, 62 skipped, 0 masked, 0 errors.
NOTE: Resolving any missing task queue dependencies

Build Configuration:
BB_VERSION        = "1.35.0"
BUILD_SYS         = "x86_64-linux"
NATIVELSBSTRING   = "universal"
TARGET_SYS        = "arm-poky-linux-gnueabi"
MACHINE           = "qemuarm"
DISTRO            = "poky"
DISTRO_VERSION    = "2.4"
TUNE_FEATURES     = "arm armv5 thumb dsp"
TARGET_FPU        = "soft"
meta
meta-poky
meta-yocto-bsp    = "rocko:65d23bd7986615fdfb0f1717b615534a2a14ab80"

Initialising tasks: 100% |##########################################################| Time: 0:00:00
NOTE: Executing RunQueue Tasks
NOTE: Tasks Summary: Attempted 2 tasks of which 0 didn't need to be rerun and all succeeded.
NOTE: Writing buildhistory
NOTE: Recipe bbexample_git.bb has been created; further editing may be required to make it fully functional
$ ▮
```

The `recipetool` creates the `bbexample_git.bb` file after downloading the source code from the URL and analyzing its content. Based on the source code it creates the base of the recipe, as shown in the following image:

```
The recipe bbexample_git.bb created by recipetool
$ cat bbexample_git.bb
# Recipe created by recipetool
# This is the basis of a recipe and may need further editing in order to be fully functional.
# (Feel free to remove these comments when editing.)

# WARNING: the following LICENSE and LIC_FILES_CHKSUM values are best guesses - it is
# your responsibility to verify that the values are complete and correct.
LICENSE = "MIT"
LIC_FILES_CHKSUM = "file://LICENSE;md5=96af5705d6f64a88e035781ef00e98a8"

SRC_URI = "git://github.com/OsSystems/bbexample;protocol=https"

# Modify these as desired
PV = "1.0+git${SRCPV}"
SRCREV = "ece3cef9abc95cb77c931f9f27860102e43cc1d9"

S = "${WORKDIR}/git"

# NOTE: if this software is not capable of being built in a separate build directory
# from the source, you should replace autotools with autotools-brokensep in the
# inherit line
inherit autotools

# Specify any options you want to pass to the configure script using EXTRA_OECONF:
EXTRA_OECONF = ""

$ ▮
```

Even though the `recipetool` creates a base recipe, it should not be taken as a final recipe. You should check for compilation options, extra metadata information, and so on.

The `bbexample_git.bb` file is created in the directory the `recipetool` is executed (`build`), we must then copy the file to the desired location, in the example `meta-newlayer/recipes-mine/bbexample/bbexample_git.bb`. After copying it, we can build it using BitBake as usual.

Adding support to a new machine definition

Creating a new machine to be used by Poky is a straightforward task. It essentially provides the information needed for a machine to work. The bootloader, kernel, and hardware support drivers must be checked before starting to integrate the board into the BSP layer.

The Yocto Project supports x86-32, x86-64, ARM32, ARM64, MIPS, MIPS64, and PowerPC, representing the most currently-used embedded architectures.

The prevailing set of variables used in a machine definition is as follows:

- `TARGET_ARCH`: This sets the machine architecture, for example, ARM and i586
- `PREFERRED_PROVIDER_virtual/kernel`: This overrides the default kernel (`linux-yocto`) in case you need to use a specific one
- `SERIAL_CONSOLES`: This defines serial consoles and their speeds
- `MACHINE_FEATURES`: This describes hardware features, so the software stack needed is included in the images by default
- `KERNEL_IMAGETYPE`: This is used to choose the kernel image type, for example, `zImage` and `uImage`
- `IMAGE_FSTYPES`: This sets the generated filesystem image types, for example, `tar.gz`, `ext4`, and `ubifs`

You can see examples of machine definition files inside the Poky source code in `meta-yocto-bsp/conf/machine/`. When describing a new machine, we should pay special attention to specific features supported by it in `MACHINE_FEATURES`. This way, the needed software to support these features is installed into the images. The current available values for `MACHINE_FEATURES` are listed as follows:

- `acpi`: Hardware has ACPI (x86/x86_64 only)

- `alsa`: Hardware has ALSA audio drivers

- `apm`: Hardware uses APM (or APM emulation)

- `bluetooth`: Hardware has integrated BT

- `efi`: Support for booting through EFI

- `ext2`: Hardware HDD or Microdrive

- irda: Hardware has IrDA support

- keyboard: Hardware has a keyboard

- pcbios: Support for booting through BIOS

- pci: Hardware has a PCI bus

- pcmcia: Hardware has PCMCIA or CompactFlash sockets

- phone: Mobile phone (voice) support

- qvga: Machine has a QVGA (320x240) display

- rtc: Machine has a real-time clock

- screen: Hardware has a screen

- serial: Hardware has serial support (usually RS232)

- touchscreen: Hardware has a touchscreen

- usbgadget: Hardware is USB gadget device compatible

- usbhost: Hardware is USB host compatible

- vfat: FAT filesystem support

- wifi: Hardware has integrated Wi-Fi

Wrapping an image for your machine

One aspect that is often neglected until the very end of any BSP support layer development is creating a ready-to-use image for the machine. The type of image we will use depends on multiple aspects: the processor, peripherals included on the board, and project restrictions.

The most frequently-used type of images for direct use on the storage is the **partitioned image**. The Yocto Project has a tool, called `wic`, which provides a flexible way to generate those images. It allows the creation of partitioned images based on a template file (`wks`) written in a common language that describes the target image layout. The language definition can be found in the documentation here: `http://www.yoctoproject.org/docs/2.4/ref-manual/ref-manual.html#openembedded-kickstart-wks-reference`.

The `wks` file is placed in our metalayer inside the `wic` directory. It is not uncommon to have in this directory multiple files to specify different image layouts; however, it is important to bear in mind that the chosen layout must match with the machine.

For example, when considering an i.MX-based machine that boots using SPL and U-Boot from an SD card with two partitions, one for the boot files and other for the `rootfs`. The respective `wks` is shown here:

```
# short-description: Create SD card image with a boot partition
# long-description:
# Create an image that can be written onto a SD card using dd for use
# with i.MX SoC family.
# It uses SPL and u-boot
#
# The disk layout used is:
#    - ----- --------- -------------- --------------
#   | | SPL | u-boot  |     boot     |     rootfs     |
#    - ----- --------- -------------- --------------
#   ^ ^      ^          ^              ^
#   | |      |          |              |
# 0 1kiB   69kiB    4MiB            16MiB + rootfs + IMAGE_EXTRA_SPACE (default
10MiB)
#
part SPL --source rawcopy --sourceparams="file=SPL" --ondisk mmcblk --no-
table --align 1
part u-boot --source rawcopy --sourceparams="file=u-boot.img" --ondisk
mmcblk --no-table --align 69
part /boot --source bootimg-partition --ondisk mmcblk --fstype=vfat --label
boot --active --align 4096 --size 16
part / --source rootfs --ondisk mmcblk --fstype=ext4 --label root --align
4096

bootloader --ptable msdos
```

To enable the Wic-based image generation, it is a matter of adding it to the `IMAGE_FSTYPES`. We can also define the `wks` file to be used by setting the `WKS_FILE` variable. Those variables are detailed at `http://www.yoctoproject.org/docs/2.4/ref-manual/ref-manual.html`

Using a custom distribution

The creation of a distribution is a mix of simplicity and complexity. The process of creating the distribution file is very easy; however, the distribution configuration has a high impact in the way Poky behaves, and may cause a binary incompatibility with previously built binaries, depending on the options we use.

The distribution is where we define global options, such as the toolchain version, graphical backends, support for OpenGL, and so on. We should make a distribution only in case the default settings provided by Poky do not fulfil our requirements.

Usually, we intend to change a small set of options from Poky. For example, we remove the X11 support to use a framebuffer instead. We can easily accomplish this by reusing Poky distribution and overriding the variables we need. For example, the sample distribution represented by the file `<layer>/conf/distro/mydistro.conf` is as follows:

```
require conf/distro/poky.conf
DISTRO = "mydistro"
DISTRO_NAME = "mydistro (My New Distro)"
DISTRO_VERSION = "1.0"
DISTRO_CODENAME = "codename"
SDK_VENDOR = "-mydistrosdk"
SDK_VERSION := "${@'${DISTRO_VERSION}'.replace('snapshot-${DATE}','snapshot')}"

MAINTAINER = "mydistro <mydistro@mycompany.com>"

DISTRO_FEATURES_remove = "x11"
```

To use the distribution just created, we need to add in the following piece of code `build/conf/local.conf`:

```
DISTRO = "mydistro"
```

The variable `DISTRO_FEATURES` may influence how the recipes are configured and the packages are installed in images. For example, if we want to be able to use sound in any machine and image, the `alsa` features must be present. The following list shows the present state for `DISTRO_FEATURES` supported values:

- `alsa:` Includes ALSA support (OSS compatibility kernel modules installed if available)

- `api-documentation:` Enables generation of API documentation during recipe builds

- `bluetooth`: Includes Bluetooth support (integrated BT only)

- `bluez5`: Includes BlueZ Version 5, which provides core Bluetooth layers and protocols support

- `cramfs`: Includes CramFS support

- `directfb`: Includes DirectFB support

- `ext2`: Includes tools for supporting devices with internal HDD/Microdrive for storing files (instead of Flash-only devices)

- `ipsec`: Includes IPSec support

- `ipv6`: Includes IPv6 support

- `irda`: Includes IrDA support

- `keyboard`: Includes keyboard support (for example, Keymaps will be loaded during boot)

- `ldconfig`: Includes support for `ldconfig` and `ld.so.conf` on the target

- `nfs`: Includes NFS client support (for mounting NFS exports onto device)

- `opengl`: Includes the **Open Graphics Library** (**OpenGL**), which is a cross-language, multi-platform application programming interface used for rendering two and three-dimensional graphics

- `pci`: Includes PCI bus support

- `pcmcia`: Includes PCMCIA/CompactFlash support

- `ppp`: Includes PPP dial-up support

- `ptest`: Enables building the package tests where supported by individual recipes

- `smbfs`: Includes SMB networks client support (for mounting Samba/Microsoft Windows shares on device)

- `systemd:` Includes support for this `init` manager, which is a full replacement for `sysvinit` with parallel starting of services, reduced shell overhead, and other features

- `usbgadget:` Includes USB gadget device support (for USB networking/serial/storage)

- `usbhost:` Includes USB host support (allows connection to external keyboard, mouse, storage, and network, among others)

- `wayland:` Includes the Wayland display server protocol and the library that supports it

- `wifi:` Includes Wi-Fi support (integrated only)

- `x11:` Includes the X server and libraries

MACHINE_FEATURES versus DISTRO_FEATURES

Both `DISTRO_FEATURES` and `MACHINE_FEATURES` work together to provide feasible support on the final system.

When a machine supports a feature, this does not imply that it is being supported by the final system because the distribution used must provide the underlying base for it.

If a machine supports Wi-Fi but the distribution does not, the applications used by the operating system will be built with Wi-Fi support disabled, so that the outcome will be a system without Wi-Fi support.

On the other hand, if the distribution provides Wi-Fi support and a machine does not, the modules and applications needed for the Wi-Fi will not be installed in images built for this machine, though the operating system and its modules have support for Wi-Fi enabled.

Understanding the variables scope

The BitBake metadata has thousands of variables, but the scope where these variables are available depends on where it is defined. Basically, there are two kinds of variables as follows:

- Variables defined in configuration files are global to every recipe. The parsing order of the main configuration files is shown as follows:
    - `build/conf/local.conf`
    - `<layer>/conf/machines/<machine>.conf`
    - `<layer>/conf/distro/<distro>.conf`
- Variables defined within recipe files are local to the specific recipe only during the execution of its tasks

Summary

In this chapter, we learned the reasons that motivate us to create a new layer and metadata. We saw a description of how to create machine configuration, a distribution definition, and recipes files. We learned how we can create images and how to include our application in an image.

In the next chapter, we will access some examples of the most common customization cases used by an additional layer, such as modifying existing packages, adding extra options to `autoconf`, applying a new patch, and including a new file to a package. We will see how to configure BusyBox and `linux-yocto`, two packages commonly customized when making an embedded system.

12
Customizing Existing Recipes

In the course of our work with Yocto Project's tools, it is expected that we will need to customize existing recipes. In this chapter, we will explore some examples, such as changing compilation options, enabling or disabling features of a recipe, applying an extra patch, and modifying **BusyBox** and **Linux Yocto Framework** settings.

Common use cases

Nowadays, projects usually have a set of layers to provide the required features. We certainly need to make changes on top of them to adapt them to our specific needs. They may be cosmetic or substantive changes, but the way to make them is the same.

To make changes to a preexisting recipe, we need to create a `.bbappend` file in our project layer. The name of the file is the same as the original recipe, along with the `append` suffix. For example, if the original recipe was named `<original-layer>/recipes-core/app/app_1.0.bb`, our respective `.bbappend` will be `<layer>/recipes-core/app/app_1.0.bbappend`.

The `.bbappend` file can be seen as a piece of text that is appended at the end of the original recipe. It empowers us with an extremely flexible mechanism to avoid duplicating source code in order to apply the required changes to our project's layers.

 When there is more than one `.bbappend` file for a recipe, all of them are joined following the layer's priority order.

Adding extra options to recipes based on Autoconf

Let's assume we have Autoconf's build system-based application, along with a preexisting recipe for it, and we want to do the following:

- Enable my-feature
- Disable another-feature

The content of the `.bbappend` file, in order to make the changes, will be the following:

```
EXTRA_OECONF += "--enable-my-feature --disable-another-feature"
EXTRA_OEMAKE += "DEFINE_PASSED_TO_MAKE=1"
```

This can also be done based on the hardware we are building for, as follows:

```
EXTRA_OECONF_append_arm = " --enable-my-arm-feature"
EXTRA_OEMAKE_append_mymachine = " MYMACHINE_SPECIFIC=1"
```

EXTRA_OECONF is used to add extra options to the configuration script. EXTRA_OEMAKE is used to add extra parameters to the make call.

Applying a patch

For cases where we need to apply a patch to an existing package, we should use FILESEXTRAPATHS, which includes new directories in the searching algorithm, making the extra file visible to BitBake, as shown here:

```
FILESEXTRAPATHS_prepend := "${THISDIR}/${PN}-${PV}:"
SRC_URI += "file://mypatch.patch"
```

In the preceding example, THISDIR expands to the current directory, and PN and PV expand to the package name and package version, respectively. This new path is then included in the directories list used for file searching. The use of the _prepend operator is important as it guarantees that our provided file is used, even if a file with the same name is added in the lower priority layers in future.

BitBake assumes that every file with a `.patch` extension is a patch and applies them accordingly.

Adding extra files to the existing packages

If we need to include an extra configuration file, we should use FILESEXTRAPATHS, as explained in the previous example and shown in the following lines of code:

```
FILESEXTRAPATHS_prepend := "${THISDIR}/${PN}-${PV}:"
SRC_URI += "file://newconfigfile.conf"
do_install_append() {
    install -m 644 ${WORKDIR}/newconfig.conf ${D}${sysconfdir}
}
```

The do_install_append function appends the provided block below the metadata already available in the original do_install function. It includes the command needed to copy our new configuration file into the package's filesystem. The file is copied from ${WORKDIR} to ${D} as these are the directories used by Poky to build the package and the destination directory used by Poky to create the package. The ${sysconfdir} directory is the system configuration directory (usually with /etc).

> We should use the variables provided on top of poky/meta/conf/bitbake.conf, instead of pointing to hardcoded paths. For example, use ${sysconfdir} instead of /etc, and ${bindir} in place of /usr/bin.

Understanding file searching paths

When a file (a patch or a generic file) is included in SRC_URI, BitBake searches for FILESPATH and FILESEXTRAPTH variables. The default setting is to look in the following locations:

- <recipe>-<version>/
- <recipe>/
- files/

As well as this, it also checks for a OVERRIDES for a specific files to be overrided in each folder. To illustrate this, consider a recipe, foo_1.0.bb, and the variable OVERRIDES = "<board>:<arch>" the file will be searched in the following directories, respecting the exact order, shown:

- foo-1.0/<board>/
- foo-1.0/<arch>/
- foo-1.0/

- `foo/<board>/`
- `foo/<arch>/`
- `foo/`
- `files/<board>/`
- `files/<arch>/`
- `files/`

This is just illustrative as the list of OVERRIDES is huge and machine-specific. When we work with our recipe, we can use `bitbake -e` in order to find out the full list of available overrides for a specific machine and use them accordingly.

Changing recipe feature configuration

One supported mechanism to simplify feature set customization for recipes is PACKAGECONFIG. It provides a way to enable and disable the recipe features. For example, say the recipe has the following configuration:

```
PACKAGECONFIG ?= "feature1"
PACKAGECONFIG[feature1] = "--enable-feature1,--disablefeature1,
feature1depends"
PACKAGECONFIG[feature2] = "--enable-feature2,--disablefeature2,
feature2depends"
```

The recipe has two features, `feature1` and `feature2`. For each configuration option, there is a string to define how to enable the feature on `autoconf`, how to disable the feature on `autoconf`, and the new dependencies in case the option is enabled.

We can create a `.bbappend` file that expands the PACKAGECONFIG variable's default value to enable `feature2` as well, as shown here:

```
PACKAGECONFIG += "feature2"
```

 In order to add the same feature to the `build/conf/local.conf` file, we can use `PACKAGECONFIG_pn-<recipename>_append = 'feature2'`.

More detailed information about the use of PACKAGECONFIG and its options can be found at `http://www.yoctoproject.org/docs/2.4/ref-manual/ref-manual.html`.

Customizing BusyBox

BusyBox is a key component of most embedded, Linux-based projects as it provides an alternative to the most commonly used utilities, but with a smaller footprint than its usual Linux counterparts. It can be seen as a sort of Swiss Army knife, since it provides a huge set of utilities and is quite flexible regarding which utilities to enable or disable.

 When we want to deselect an option, we can add a negative line instead, for example, `CONFIG_TFTPD=n`.

Poky provides a default setting for BusyBox, and it may sometimes not fulfill our needs, so changing this configuration is a common task. For example, the `<layer>/recipes-core/busybox/busybox_%.bbappend` file could have the following lines of code:

```
FILESEXTRAPATHS_prepend := "${THISDIR}/${PN}:"
SRC_URI += "file://enable-tftpd.cfg"
```

The `<layer>/recipes-core/busybox/busybox/enable-tftpd.cfg` file contains the following:

```
CONFIG_TFTPD=y
```

This combination of the `.bbappend` file and configuration file is enough to enable support for the **TFTP** server in BusyBox.

 When a `.bbappend` file is created, the `%` operator is used as a wildcard (such as in the `<layer>/recipes-core/busybox/busybox_%.bbappend` example) and the `.bbappend` file will be appended to any original recipe metadata.

Customizing the linux-yocto framework

The Linux kernel is a complex piece of software that provides an infinite number of possible configurations. The Yocto Project provides a framework (`linux-yocto`) to manage a huge set of machines in a single kernel tree. We can take advantage of this framework to enable or disable features for your machine, for example, by using `<layer>/recipes-kernel/linux/linux-yocto_%.bbappend` with the following content:

```
FILESEXTRAPATHS_prepend := "${THISDIR}/${PN}:"
SRC_URI += "file://enable-can.cfg"
```

The content of the `<layer>/recipes-kernel/linux/linux-yocto/linux-yocto/enable-can.cfg` file is shown here:

```
CONFIG_CAN=y
```

One common requirement when creating a Linux-based embedded system is to change the kernel configuration. We can do this using the SDK or BitBake, as explained here:

- **Using the SDK**: The creation and installation of the Yocto Project's SDK is detailed in `Chapter 8`, *Developing with the Yocto Project*. After having the SDK exported, we can configure the Linux kernel source in the usual way (for example, `make menuconfig`).
- **Using BitBake**: When small changes or testing is needed, we can use BitBake to configure or generate the Linux kernel configuration file. We can use the following commands to achieve this:

```
$ bitbake virtual/kernel -c menuconfig
$ bitbake virtual/kernel -c savedefconfig
```

For Linux kernel development, the use of SDK is preferred as it provides a convenient development environment; BitBake should be used only for quick changes.

We need to bear in mind that not every supported machine in the Yocto Project, vendor, and community BSP layers uses the `linux-yocto` framework. This means that the configuration fragment mechanism is not available for those machines, and we need to provide a full `defconfig` file in order to customize their kernel.

The complete `linux-yocto` documentation can be found, which covers all aspects of the `linux-yocto` framework and advanced Linux kernel maintenance concepts.

We can use `recipetool` to help us with the `.bbappend` creation procedure by using a command line such as `$ recipetool newappend -w -e ../meta-newlayer bc` to create a `.bbappend` file on top of the current version of `bc`.

Summary

In this chapter, we learned how we can customize existing recipes using the `.bbappend` files and benefit from this by avoiding the duplication source code. We saw how to enable or disable one feature, how to apply a patch, and how to change BusyBox and the `linux-yocto` framework's configuration.

In the next chapter, we will discuss how the Yocto Project can help us with some legal aspects of producing a Linux-based system using packages under different licenses. We will understand which artifacts we need and how Poky can be configured to generate the artifacts that should be shared as part of the copyleft compliance accomplishment process.

13
Achieving GPL Compliance

In this chapter, we will see how we can ensure open source license compliance and how we can use Poky to provide the artifacts needed, such as the source code, licensing text, and the list of derivative work. This is critical for most products that are introduced into the market nowadays, as open source code needs to live side by side with proprietary code.

Understanding copyleft

Copyleft is a legal way to use copyright law in order to maximize rights and express freedom. It greatly impacts our day-to-day work to such a large extent that companies must know how to deal with open source and free software licenses, as they have a big impact on their products.

When building a Linux distribution, there are at least two projects being used: the Linux kernel and a compiler. The most commonly used compiler nowadays is the **GNU Compiler Collection (GCC)**.

The Linux kernel is released under the **GPLv2** license, and the GCC is released under the **GPLv2**, **GPLv2.1**, and **GPLv3** licenses, depending on the project used.

However, a Linux-based system can include virtually all projects available throughout the world, in addition to all applications made by the company for its product. How do we know the number of projects and licenses that are included, and how do we fulfill copyleft compliance requirements?

 This chapter describes how the Yocto Project can help you in the task, but be aware that you must know exactly what you need to provide and the possible license incompatibilities. If you have any doubts, please consult your legal department or a copyright lawyer.

In this chapter, we will look at how the Yocto Project can help us with the most common tasks required for copyleft compliance.

Copyleft compliance versus proprietary code

It is important to understand that proprietary code and copyleft-covered code can coexist in the same product. We need to be careful about the libraries we link the code with because some may have license compatibility issues. However, this is the standard in most of the products available in the market nowadays.

Some guidelines for license compliance

As already mentioned, one Linux-based system is a set of several projects, each one under a different license. The Yocto Project helps developers understand that most copyleft project obligations have the following conditions:

- The source code of the project must be provided along with the binary
- The license of the project must be provided along with the binary
- Any modification to the project or any script that is needed to configure and build it must be provided along with the binary

That means that if one project under copyleft is modified, then the license text, the base source code, and any modification must be included in the final deliverable.

The assumptions cover most rights guaranteed by copyleft licenses. These are the parts where the Yocto Project can help us. However, before releasing anything, it is recommended that we audit all the materials to be released to make sure they're complete.

Managing software licensing with Poky

One important Poky feature is the ability to manage licenses. Most of the time, we, as developers, do not care about licenses because we keep our focus on our own bugs. However, when creating a product, it is very important to care and know about licenses and the kinds of licenses present in the product.

Poky keeps track of licenses, works with commercial and noncommercial licenses, and has a strategy to work with proprietary applications, at least during the development cycle.

One important thing to know, at first, is that a recipe is released under a certain license, and it represents a project released under a different license. The recipe and the project are two different entities and they have different licensing, so the two different licenses must be considered part of the product.

In most recipes, information is a comment containing the copyright, license, and author name; this information pertains to the recipe itself. Then, there is a set of variables to describe the package license, and they are as follows:

- LICENSE: This describes the license under which the package was released.
- LIC_FILES_CHKSUM: This may not seem very useful at first sight. It describes the license file and its checksum for a certain package, and we may find a lot of variation in how a project describes its license. The most common license files are stored in meta/files/common-licenses/.

Some projects include a file, such as COPYING or LICENSE, which specifies the license for the source code. Others use a header note in each file or in the main file. The LIC_FILES_CHKSUM variable has the checksum for the license text of a project; if any letters are changed, the checksum is changed as well. This is used to make sure any change is noted and consciously accepted by the developer. A license change may be a typo fix; however, it may also be a change in legal obligations, so it is important for the developer to review and understand the change.

When a different license checksum is detected, BitBake launches a build error and points to the project that had its license changed. You must be careful when this happens as the license change may impact the use of this software. In order to be able to build anything again, you must change the LIC_FILE_CHKSUM value accordingly, and update the LICENSE field to match the license change. Your legal department should be consulted if the license terms have changed.

Commercial licenses

By default, Poky does not install any package with a commercial license restriction. The most commonly used example is the gstreamer1.0-plugins-ugly package. This is archived though a variable used on these recipes with some license restriction; the LICENSE_FLAGS variable is used to determine the restriction.

In the case of gstreamer1.0-plugins-ugly, the variable in the recipe is set to LICENSE_FLAGS = "commercial", although it may have a string. Some projects choose to set it to LICENSE_FLAGS = "<license>_${PN}_${PV}".

In order to install these recipes, we must place a whitelist of desired special licensing in `build/conf/local.conf`, and we can do this using `LICENSE_FLAGS_WHITELIST`. This variable determines the special license that can be used, and has very flexible content.

For example, for GStreamer Ugly plug-ins, we may only want this package to be installed, so we add the following variable in `build/conf/local.conf`:

```
LICENSE_FLAGS_WHITELIST_pn-gstreamer1.0-plugins-ugly = "commercial"
```

This allows the use of `gstreamer1.0-plugins-ugly` while excluding any other commercial recipe, such as `gstreamer1.0-plugins-bad`. However, if we want BitBake to install any commercial package from our image, we may use the following code in `build/conf/local.conf`:

```
LICENSE_FLAGS_WHITELIST = "commercial"
```

Using Poky to achieve copyleft compliance

At this point, we know how to use Poky and understand its main goal. It is time to understand the legal aspects of producing a Linux-based system that uses packages under different licenses.

We can configure Poky to generate the artifacts that should be shared as part of the copyleft compliance process.

License auditing

To help us to achieve copyleft compliance, Poky generates a license manifest during the image build, located at `build/tmp/deploy/licenses/<image_name-machine_name-datestamp>/`.

To demonstrate this process, we will use the `core-image-full-cmdline` image for the `qemuarm` machine. To start with our example, look at the files under `build/tmp/deploy/licenses/core-image-full-cmdline-qemuarm-<datastamp>`, which are as follows:

- `image_license.manifest`: This lists the recipe names, versions, licenses, and the files of packages that are available in `build/tmp/deploy/image/<machine>` but not installed inside `rootfs`. The most common examples are the bootloader, the Linux kernel image, and DTB files.

- `package.manifest`: This lists all the packages in the image.
- `license.manifest`: This lists the names, versions, recipe names, and licenses for all the installed packages. This file may be used for copyleft compliance auditing.

Providing the source code

The most obvious way Poky can help us to provide the source code of every project used in our image is by sharing the `DL_DIR` content. However, this approach has one important pitfall: Any proprietary source code will be shared within `DL_DIR` if it is shared as is. In addition, this approach will share any source code, including parts that are not required by copyleft compliance.

Another way is to configure Poky to generate the set of source codes and decide what will be delivered. This may be done using the `archiver` class. This class copies the source code for each package under the `build/tmp/deploy` folder, separated by architecture (in our example, the present architectures are `allarch-poky-linux`, `arm-poky-linux-gnueabi`, and `x86_64-linux`) and license. The package for `armpoky-linux-gnueabi`, released under GPLv3, is placed in the `build/tmp/deploy/sources/arm-poky-linux-gnueabi/GPLv3/package-name` directory.

Poky must be configured to archive the source code before the final image is created. So, in order to have it, we can paste the following variables into `build/conf/local.conf`:

```
INHERIT += "archiver"
ARCHIVER_MODE[src] = "original"
```

Keep in mind that, even with this approach, if we share the `build/tmp/deploy/sources` directories, the proprietary sources are shared, even though this is unnecessary, although we may now choose to share the source based on licensing. We can copy only the packages under GPLv3 or MIT to a shareable place, or to any other combination of licensing, according to the desired sharing strategy.

One example of a copy command line, used to copy all packages under any GPL license (from: `http://www.yoctoproject.org/docs/2.4/dev-manual/dev-manual.html`), is the following:

```
# Script to archive a subset of packages matching specific license(s)
# Source and license files are copied into sub folders of package folder
# Must be run from build folder
#!/bin/bash
src_release_dir="source-release"
```

```
mkdir -p $src_release_dir
for a in tmp/deploy/sources/*; do
    for d in $a/*; do
        Get package name from path
        p=`basename $d`
        p=${p%-*}
        p=${p%-*}
        # Only archive GPL packages (update *GPL* regex for your license
check)
        numfiles=`ls tmp/deploy/licenses/$p/*GPL* 2> /dev/null | wc -l`
        if [ $numfiles -gt 1 ]; then
            echo Archiving $p
            mkdir -p $src_release_dir/$p/source
            cp $d/* $src_release_dir/$p/source 2> /dev/null
            mkdir -p $src_release_dir/$p/license
            cp tmp/deploy/licenses/$p/* $src_release_dir/$p/license 2>
/dev/null
        fi
    done
done
```

If we prefer to get some help from Poky regarding which license must have our attention, we can add the `ARCHIVER_MODE[filter] ?= "yes"` code to `build/conf/local.conf`. The default configuration is to have the source code for every project, in other words no filter. However, if we prefer to have only the source code of `COPYLEFT_LICENSE_INCLUDE` projects, we can use a filter.

The `COPYLEFT_LICENSE_INCLUDE` variable currently includes all licenses starting with GPL or LGPL. This variable can be overridden in `build/conf/local.conf` if we wish to make sure to include another license or variation.

Providing compilation scripts and source code modifications

With the configuration provided in the previous section, Poky will package the original source code for each project. In case we want to include the patched source code, we will only use `ARCHIVER_MODE[src] = "patched"`; this way, Poky will wrap the project source code after the `do_patch` task. It includes modifications from recipes or the `bbappend` file.

This way, the source code and any modification can be shared easily. However, there is still one kind of information that has not been created so far: the procedure used to configure and build the project.

In order to have a reproducible build environment, we can share the configured project, in other words, the project after the `do_configure` task. For this, we can add the following to `build/conf/local.conf`:

```
ARCHIVER_MODE[src] = "configured"
```

It is important to remember that we must consider that the person on the other side may not use the Yocto Project for copyleft compliance; alternatively, if they are using it, they must know that the modification made to the original source code and configuration procedure is not available. This is why we share the configured project: It allows anyone to reproduce our build environment.

For all flavors of source code, the default resulting file is a tarball; other options will add `ARCHIVER_MODE[srpm] = "1"` to `build/conf/local.conf`, and the resulting file will be an SRPM package.

Providing license text

When providing the source code, the license text is shared inside it. If we want the license text inside our final image, we can add the following to `build/conf/local.conf`:

```
COPY_LIC_MANIFEST = "1"
COPY_LIC_DIRS = "1"
```

This way, the license files will be placed inside the root filesystem, under `/usr/share/common-licenses/`.

Summary

In this chapter, we learned how Poky can help with copyleft license compliance and also learned why it should not be used as a legal background. Poky enables us to generate source code, reproduction scripts, and license text for packages used in our distribution. In addition, we learned that the license manifest generated within the image may be used to audit the image.

In the next chapter, we will learn how we can use Yocto Project's tools with real hardware. We will use the Yocto Project to generate an image for use with the Beagle Bone Black, Raspberry Pi, and Wandboard machines.

14
Booting Our Custom Embedded Linux

It's time! We are now ready to boot our custom-made embedded Linux, as we have learned the required concepts and gained enough knowledge about the Yocto Project and Poky. In this chapter, we will practice what we have learned so far about using Poky with external BSP layers, use it to generate an image for use with BeagleBone Black, Raspberry Pi 3, and Wandboard machines, and boot it using the SD card.

The same concepts can be applied to every other board, as long as the vendor provides a BSP layer to use with the Yocto Project.

We will see a list of the most commonly used BSP layers in this chapter. This should not be taken as a complete list, or as a definitive one, but we want to facilitate your search for the needed layer in case you have one board of a specific vendor next to you. This list is as follows, in alphabetic order:

- **Allwinner**: This has the meta-allwinner layer
- **BeagleBoard**: This has the meta-ti layer
- **CuBox-i**: This has the meta-freescale-3rdparty layer
- **Intel**: This has the meta-intel layer
- **Raspberry Pi**: This has the meta-raspberrypi layer
- **Texas Instruments**: This has the meta-ti layer
- **Wandboard**: This has the meta-freescale-3rdparty layer

Exploring the boards

To ease the exploration of the Yocto Project's capabilities, it is good to have a real board so we can enjoy the experience of booting our customized embedded system. For such, we have tried to collect the most commonly used and widely available boards so the chances of you owning one are higher.

This chapter will cover the steps for the following boards:

- **BeagleBone Black**: The BeagleBone Black is community based, with members all around the world. Further information is available at `https://beagleboard.org/black/`.
- **Raspberry Pi 3**: The most famous ARM-based board, with the widest community gathered around the world. See more information at `https://www.raspberrypi.org/`.
- **Wandboard**: The Wandboard is supported by the Wandboard community. More information is available at `http://www.wandboard.org/`.

All the boards listed are maintained by non-profitable organizations based on education and mentoring, which makes the community a fertile place to discover the world of embedded Linux. The following figure summarizes the boards and their main features:

Board version	Features
BeagleBone Black	TI AM335x (single-core) 512MB DDR3 RAM
Raspberry Pi 3	Broadcom BCM2837 64bit CPU (quad-core) 1 GB RAM 802.11ac wireless and Bluetooth
Wandboard Solo	NXP i.MX6S processor (single-core) 512 MB RAM
Wandboard Dual	NXP i.MX6DL processor (dual-core) 1 GB RAM 802.11ac wireless and Bluetooth
Wandboard Quad	NXP i.MX6Q processor (quad-core) 2 GB RAM 802.11ac wireless and Bluetooth SATA

Wandboard QuadPlus	NXP i.MX6QP processor (quad-core) 2 GB RAM 802.11ac wireless and Bluetooth SATA

Discovering the right BSP layer

In `Chapter 10`, *Exploring External Layer*, we learned that the Yocto Project allows for the split of its metadata among different layers. It organizes the metadata so we can choose which exact meta layer to add to our project.

The way to find the BSP for a board varies, but generally we can find it by visiting `http://layers.openembedded.org/`. We can search for the machine name and the website finds on its database which layer contains it.

In the next sections, we will describe the steps needed to go from source code to the final binary to be copied to the board. Feel free to skip a section if the board isn't available to you.

Baking for the hardware

After discovering the BSP layer for the hardware we are going to use for the build, we need to download all of the needed meta layers and create the build environment.

Before starting this, we need to make sure all system requirements are met. We discussed these requirements in `Chapter 2`, *Baking Our Poky-Based System*.

The use of meta layers forces us to deal with many Git repositories of metadata. One good way to avoid confusion is putting all of the sources related to those meta layers in a specific directory. The following figure shows an example of this:

```
 ⊛  −  ◻  Terminal
├── build
└── sources
    ├── meta-freescale
    ├── meta-freescale-3rdparty
    ├── meta-openembedded
    ├── meta-raspberrypi
    ├── meta-ti
    └── poky

8 directories, 0 files
$ █
```

It is advisable to keep the layers inside the sources up to date, as it brings security fixes, bug fixes, and new features.

There are multiple ways of managing the multiple layers when making a product. One option is to use the `combo-layer` (`https://wiki.yoctoproject.org/wiki/Combo-layer`), which replicates the commits onto a single Git tree, as well as `git submodules` and `repo` to manage multiple Git repositories in a more convenient way. When using `repo`, there are approaches to facilitate it for long-term projects, for example the creation of a manifest file which lists all the meta layers to clone, see `http://doc.ossystems.com.br/managing-platforms.html` on how to create the `repo` structure. Which approach to use to organize the metadata is a personal preference, and the option of having all the meta layer Git repositories only manually cloned on the tree is a good option for simple use cases.

In the next sections, we are going to create the structure for the three boards referenced in this book.

Baking for BeagleBone Black

In order to add this board support to our project, we need to include the `meta-ti` meta layer, which is the BSP layer with support for several TI boards, including the BeagleBone Black, but not limited to this. The meta layer can be accessed at `http://git.yoctoproject.org/cgit/cgit.cgi/meta-ti`.

To create the source structure, please run the following command lines:

```
$ mkdir sources
$ cd sources
$ git clone --branch rocko git://git.yoctoproject.org/poky
$ git clone --branch rocko git://git.yoctoproject.org/meta-ti
```

The final directory structure you should have is shown in the following figure:

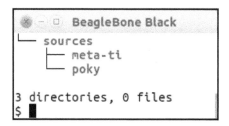

After completing this, we must create the `build` directory we use for our builds and add the BSP layer. We can do this using the following command lines:

```
$ cd ..
$ source sources/poky/oe-init-build-env build
$ bitbake-layers add-layer ../sources/meta-ti
```

After we have the `build` directory and the BSP layers properly set up, we can start the build. Inside the `build` directory, we must call the following command:

```
$ MACHINE=beaglebone bitbake <image>
```

The `MACHINE` variable can be changed depending on the board we want to use or set in `build/conf/local.conf`.

If we want to build `core-image-sato`, which provides an embedded graphical environment, we should run the following command:

```
$ MACHINE=beaglebone bitbake core-image-sato
```

Baking for Raspberry Pi 3

In order to add this board support to our project, we need to include the `meta-raspberrypi` meta layer, which is the BSP layer with support for the Raspberry Pi boards, including the Raspberry Pi 3, but not limited to this. The meta layer can be accessed at `http://git.yoctoproject.org/cgit.cgi/meta-raspberrypi`.

To create the source structure, please run the following command lines:

```
$ mkdir sources
$ cd sources
$ git clone --branch rocko git://git.yoctoproject.org/poky
$ git clone --branch rocko git://git.yoctoproject.org/meta-raspberrypi
$ git clone --branch rocko git://git.openembedded.org/meta-openembedded
```

The final directory structure you should have is shown in the following figure:

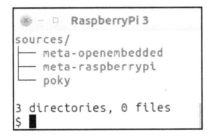

After completing this, we must create the `build` directory we use for our builds and add the BSP layer. We can do this using the following command lines:

```
$ cd ..
$ source sources/poky/oe-init-build-env build
$ bitbake-layers add-layer ../sources/meta-openembedded/meta-oe
$ bitbake-layers add-layer ../sources/meta-openembedded/meta-python
$ bitbake-layers add-layer ../sources/meta-raspberrypi
```

After we have the `build` directory and the BSP layers are properly set up, we can start the build. Inside the `build` directory, we must call the following command:

```
$ MACHINE=raspberrypi3 bitbake <image>
```

The `MACHINE` variable can be changed depending on the board we want to use or set in `build/conf/local.conf`.

If we want to build `core-image-sato`, which provides an embedded graphical environment, we should run the following command:

```
$ MACHINE=raspberrypi3 bitbake core-image-sato
```

Baking for the Wandboard

In order to add this board support to our project, we need to include the `meta-freescale-3rdparty` meta layer, which is the BSP layer with support for the Wandboard, but not limited to this. The meta layer can be accessed at `https://github.com/Freescale/meta-freescale-3rdparty`.

The `meta-freescale-3rdparty` depends on the `meta-freescale` meta layer, so we need to add both to our project.

To create the source structure, please run the following command lines:

```
$ mkdir sources
$ cd sources
$ git clone --branch rocko git://git.yoctoproject.org/poky
$ git clone --branch rocko
https://github.com/Freescale/meta-freescale-3rdparty.git
$ git clone --branch rocko git://git.yoctoproject.org/meta-freescale.git
```

The final directory structure you should have is shown in the following figure:

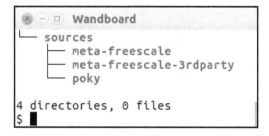

After completing this, we must create the build directory we use for our builds and add the BSP layer. We can do this using the following command lines:

```
$ cd ..
$ source sources/poky/oe-init-build-env build
$ bitbake-layers add-layer ../sources/meta-freescale
$ bitbake-layers add-layer ../sources/meta-freescale-3rdparty
```

Some packages included in NXP ARM BSP have a proprietary property and are followed by an **end-user license agreement** (**EULA**) that shows the legal impact of using it. Mainly, the GPU drivers, VPU/IPU codecs, and the `meta-freescale` layer have an EULA file that describes the rights and obligations to use the binaries and source. Read more on the EULA and in case you accept it, edit the `build/conf/local.conf` file in order to set `ACCEPT_FSL_EULA` to 1, as shown in the following line of code:

```
ACCEPT_FSL_EULA = "1"
```

This is not required for the board to work, but for full use, the hardware features are indispensable.

After we have the `build` directory and the BSP layers are properly set up, we can start the build. Inside the `build` directory, we must call the following command:

```
$ MACHINE=wandboard bitbake <image>
```

The `MACHINE` variable can be changed depending on the board we want to use or set in `build/conf/local.conf`.

If we want to build `core-image-sato`, which provides an embedded graphical environment, we should run the following command:

```
$ MACHINE=wandboard bitbake core-image-sato
```

Booting our baked image

The build process will likely take some time. There is a huge amount of work being done behind the scenes but it is a straightforward process.

After the build finishes, we need to deploy the generated image to the board, this is a process that varies from one board to another. We will cover the instructions for each board in the following sections.

Booting BeagleBone Black from the SD card

After the build process is over, the image will be available inside the `build/tmp/deploy/images/beaglebone/` directory. There are many files, but the Texas Instrument BSP generates a ready-to-use SD card image.

The file we want to use is `core-image-sato-beaglebone.wic`.

Make sure you point to the right device and double check to not write in your hard disk.

In order to copy the `core-image-sato` image to the SD card, we should use the `dd` utility, as follows:

```
$ sudo dd if=core-image-sato-beaglebone.wic of=/dev/sdX bs=1M
```

After copying the content to the SD card, insert it into the SD card slot, connect the HDMI cable, and power on the machine. It should boot nicely.

Booting Raspberry Pi 3 from the SD card

After the build process is over, the image will be available inside the `build/tmp/deploy/images/raspberrypi3/` directory. There are many files, but the Raspeberry Pi BSP generates a ready-to-use SD card image.

The file we want to use is `core-image-sato-raspberrypi3.rpi-sdimg`.

Make sure you point to the right device and double check to not write in your hard disk.

In order to copy the `core-image-sato` image to the SD card, we should use the `dd` utility, as follows:

```
$ sudo dd if=core-image-sato-raspberrypi3.rpi-sdimg of=/dev/sdX bs=1M
```

After copying the content to the SD card, insert it into the SD card slot, connect the HDMI cable, and power on the machine. It should boot nicely.

Booting Wandboard from the SD card

After the build process is over, the image will be available inside the `build/tmp/deploy/images/wandboard/` directory. There are many files, but NXP ARM BSP generates a ready-to-use SD card image.

The file we want to use is `core-image-sato-wandboard.wic.gz`.

Make sure you point to the right device and double check to not write in your hard disk.

In order to copy the `core-image-sato` image to the SD card, we should use the `dd` utility, as follows:

```
$ gunzip core-image-sato-wandboard.wic.gz
$ sudo dd if=core-image-sato-wandboard.wic of=/dev/sdX bs=1M
```

After copying the content to the SD card, insert it into the SD card slot, connect the HDMI cable, and power on the machine. It should boot nicely.

There are two SD card slots in a Wandboard. The primary slot is located in the CPU board, used for booting, and a secondary slot is found in the peripheral board (the base board).

Next steps

Pheew! We got it done! Now you should know the basics of the Yocto Project build system and be capable of extending your knowledge about it to cover other areas with much less hassle. We tried to cover the most common tasks in daily work using the Yocto Project, and there are few things you might want to practice:

- Creating `bbappend` files to apply patches or do other changes on a recipe
- Make your custom images
- Change the Linux kernel configuration file (`defconfig`)
- Change the `busybox` configuration and include the configuration fragments to add or remove a feature in a layer
- Add a new recipe for a package
- Make a product layer with your product-specific machines, recipes, and images

Remember, the source code is the ultimate knowledge source, so use it. When looking for how to do something, finding a similar recipe buys you a lot of time testing different approaches to solve the problem.

Eventually, you'll likely see yourself in a position to fix or enhance something on OpenEmbedded-Core, a meta layer, or in a BSP. Don't be afraid, and send the patches and take the feedback and requests for changes as an opportunity to learn and improve your way of solving a problem.

Summary

In this final chapter, we learned how to discover the BSP for a board we want to use in our project. We consolidated our Yocto Project knowledge by adding external BSP layers and using these in real boards with a generated image.

Throughout the book, we learned the necessary background information for you to learn any other aspect of the Yocto Project that you may need on your own. You have a general understanding of what is happening behind the scenes when you ask BitBake to build a recipe or an image. From now on, you are ready to free your mind and try new things. There are plenty of boards available, waiting for you to give them life. The ball is in your court now; here's where the fun begins!

Index

A

Allwinner 131
ARM Versatile Platform Baseboard 48

B

baked image
  booting 138
base package recipe
  creating, recipetool used 105, 107
bbexample
  reference 105
BeagleBoard 131
BeagleBone Black
  baking for 135
  booting, from SD card 139
  reference 132, 135
BitBake
  about 31
  providing 35
  reference 32, 66
  using 9
Board Support Package (BSP) 10, 93
boards
  exploring 132
BSP layer
  discovering 133
  reference 133
build directory
  constructing 46
  detailing 45
build environment
  preparing 16
Build History mechanism 84
BusyBox
  about 115
  customizing 119

C

combo-layer
  reference 134
commercial licenses 125
copyleft 123
copyleft compliance, achieving
  compilation scripts, providing 128
  license auditing 126
  license text, providing 129
  source code modifications, providing 128
  source code, providing 127
copyleft compliance
  achieving, with Poky 126
  versus proprietary code 124
CuBox-i 131
custom distribution
  using 111, 113

D

Debian
  Poky, installing 14
dependencies 34
development shell
  utilizing 87
DNF package manager 54

E

Eclipse
  integrating with Poky SDK 80, 81
end-user license agreement (EULA) 138
existing packages
  extra files, adding 117
  file searching paths 117
Extensible SDK (eSDK)
  reference 78
external layers

flexibility use 91, 92, 93

F

Fedora
   Poky, installing 14

G

gdbserver
   reference 89
generic SDK 78
global namespace
   Python functions, defining 72
GNU Compiler Collection (GCC) 123
GNU Project Debugger (GDB)
   about 89
   using, for debugging 89
GPLv2 license
   about 123
   GPLv2.1 123
   GPLv3 123

H

hardware
   baking for 133
host system
   configuring 13
   reference 14

I

image-based SDK
   using 76, 77
image
   building, to QEMU 23, 29
   creating 102
   executing, in Quick EMUlator (QEMU) 18
   tracking 84
   wrapping, for machine 109
Intel 131

L

layer
   creating 99, 101
   metadata, adding 101
   reference 99

source code, detailing 94, 95
license compliance
   guidelines 124
Linux Kernel Archive
   reference 8
linux-yocto framework
   about 115
   customizing 119, 120
   customizing, with BitBake 120
   customizing, with SDK 120
local.conf file
   knowing 16
logging functions
   in Python 86
   in Shell Script 86

M

MACHINE_FEATURES
   versus DISTRO_FEATURES 113
meta layers
   adding 96, 97
meta-toolchain 78
metadata
   and application debugging, difference 83
   basic variable setting 66
   classes 65
   configuration 65
   exploring 32
   meta-poky 10
   meta-yocto-bsp 10
   parsing 33
   recipes 65
   using 65
   working with 66

N

new machine definition
   support, adding 108

O

OpenEmbedded Layer index
   reference 96
OpenEmbedded Project 10
OpenEmbedded-Core 10

P

package feeds
  about 59
  using 61, 62
package recipe
  adding 104
package versioning 58
package
  tracking 84
packaging
  debugging 85
partitioned image 110
patch
  applying 116
Poky SDK
  and Eclipse integration 80, 81
  applications, developing on target system 79, 80
  generic SDK, creating 78
  image-based SDK, suing 76, 77
  using 78
  working with 76
Poky
  about 9
  classes, reference 104
  external layers, flexibility use 91
  installing, on Debian 14
  installing, on Fedora 14
  source code, downloading 15
  used, for achieving copyleft compliance 126
  used, for managing software licensing 124
Python
  variable expansion 71

Q

Quality Assurance (QA) 10
Quick EMUlator (QEMU)
  image, building 23, 29
  images, executing 18

R

Raspberry Pi 131
Raspberry Pi 3
  baking for 136
  booting, from SD card 139

  reference 132, 136
reasons, for disabling network access
  build decoupling 40
  network cost 40
  policy 40
  shortage 40
recipe feature configuration
  modifying 118
recipes, based on Autoconf
  extra options, adding 116
recipes
  preferring 35
recipetool
  used, for creating base package recipe 105, 107
repo structure
  reference 134
root filesystem image
  generating 42, 43
runtime package
  dependencies, specifying 58

S

SDK contents
  tracking 84
shared state cache 57
software development kit (SDK)
  deciphering 75, 76
software licensing
  managing, with Poky 124
source code
  download, optimizing 38
  fetching 36
  Git repositories 37
  network access, disabling 40
  remote file, downloading 36
supported package formats
  Debian Package Manager (DEB) 53
  installation, code execution 55, 56
  IPK 54
  OpenMoko 54
  RPM 53
  selecting 54
  TAR 54
  using 53
sysroot directories 50, 52

T

target image
  building 17
target system
  applications, developing 79, 80
task execution
  information, logging 86
tasks, BitBake
  about 40
  extending 42
tasks, build directory
  configuring and building 46
  fetching 46
  installing 46
  packages, creating 46
  source preparation 46
  sysroot, wrapping 46
temporary build directory
  exploring 47
Texas Instruments 131
Toaster
  about 21
  accessing 22
  installing 22
  reference 22
  using, hosted way 21
  using, local instance 21

U

use cases 115

V

variable
  appending operators 68
  conditional appending 70
  conditional metadata set 69
  default value, setting with ?= operator 67
  default value, setting with ??= operator 67
  executable metadata, defining 71
  expanding 66
  file inclusion 70
  inheritance system 72
  prepending operators 68
  scope 114
  syntax operators, overriding 69

W

Wandboard
  about 131
  baking for 137
  booting, from SD card 139
  reference 132, 137
WKS_FILE variable
  reference 110
work directory 48, 50

Y

Yocto Project
  about 7, 11
  delineating 8
  layer ecosystem 97, 98
  reference 57, 85, 110
  steps 140

www.ingramcontent.com/pod-product-compliance
Lightning Source LLC
Chambersburg PA
CBHW080534060326
40690CB00022B/5120